BEAUTIFUL THINGS TO
MAKE FOR BRIDES

CONTENTS

EDITORIAL
Fairfax Press
Craft Editor: Tonia Todman
Food Editor: Sheryle Eastwood
Managing Editor: Judy Poulos
Editor: Marian Broderick
Editorial Coordinator: Margaret Kelly
Text: Mary Jane Bailey
Assistant Craft Editor: Sally Pereira
Assistant Food Editor: Rachel Blackmore
Sewing and craft assistance: Martina Oprey,
Yvonne Deacon, Louise Pfanner, Gill Fury, Kate
Fury, Suzanne Lynch
Australian Editorial Coordinators: Claire Pallant,
Nadia Sbisa

DESIGN AND PRODUCTION
Sheridan Carter
Kirsten Tona
Chris Hatcher
Barbara Martusewicz

ILLUSTRATIONS
Kim Bywater

PHOTOGRAPHY
Andrew Elton
Food Styling: Carolyn Fienberg

PUBLISHER
Philippa Sandall

Family Circle
Editorial Director: Carol A. Guasti
Editorial Production Coordinator: Celeste Bantz
Project Editor: Leslie Gilbert Elman
Craft Editors: Arlene Gise, Toni Scott
Food Editor: Jo Ann Brett

Beautiful Things to Make for Brides
Includes Index
ISBN 0-937769-18-5

Formatted by J.B. Fairfax Press Pty Ltd
Printed by Toppan Printing Co. Hong Kong

BRIDE TO BE

A wedding is a very special event for the bride-to-be, her family and good friends. This book is full of wonderful ideas for making the occasion even more memorable by adding the very personal touch that comes from the work of loving hands. It's not the spectacular but the small details, often handmade, that give a wedding its atmosphere and style.

The projects and recipes in this book will help add a touch of individuality to all the time-honored wedding traditions – the invitations, wedding ceremony and reception, and the thank-you notes. From planning the menu to crafting headpieces for the attendants and to choosing flowers for the bridal bouquet, we've assembled dozens of valuable ideas and instructions for the bride, her family and friends who want to create a very personalized wedding celebration.

Especially for the bride, we've provided guidelines for wedding etiquette, calculating wedding and honeymoon budgets and selecting the perfect gown. We've even added imaginative suggestions for setting up a first home. Friends and family will love our patterns and recipes for shower gifts and tokens to make for the bride – from preserves and condiments to fill her pantry shelves to ruffled and embroidered luxuries for a romantic trousseau. A wedding should be a unique and personal expression of love for the bride and groom. Use our ideas as inspiration for making plans, and creating gowns, bouquets and wedding cakes with a confident and imaginative hand.

HERE COMES THE
BRIDE

*Getting married can be quite a complicated business. Use
this simple guide to steer you smoothly, step by step, through
the necessary arrangements and legal requirements.
Our Bridal Calendar and Budget will provide you with
helpful pointers for your wedding plans.*

Congratulations! You're about to begin planning your wedding – one of the most important events of your life. For many women, this is an extremely emotional and exciting time. There is much to do and seemingly little time to do it. The better prepared you are for the months ahead, the easier and more enjoyable they will be.

You've already accomplished the most difficult part of planning your wedding: you've found a man you love and trust enough to marry. In the coming months, your fiance will be an important part of your support system. Be patient with each other and work together on your wedding plans. Remember, the big day is for both of you.

As the bride, you are the focal point of the wedding. You may already have a vision of what you want to wear, how the ceremony will flow and even what the food at the reception will be. Understandably, you want your wedding to be as close to your vision as possible. But remember, you fiance may also have thoughts about what he would like to wear or where he would like the ceremony to take place, (you might be surprised by how much thought men give to their weddings). Your parents and your future in-laws will also have ideas and opinons about what

*With this ring
I thee wed ...*

Photography by Alan Khan and Christopher Poulos

your wedding should be.

Be gracious and be accommodating. It might help for everyone to write a list of their priorities. With luck, you'll be able to include suggestions from all fronts in your wedding plans. You might find that planning your wedding will be a severe test of your tact and diplomacy. You're sure to rise to the occasion.

WHERE TO START
Where? When? How? Who?

Thinking about wedding details can make your head spin! The best way to begin planning is by consulting someone with experience.

Your **clergyman** can be a great help. He can outline the procedures and rules for marriage specified by your religion and by state or local law. He can explain the protocol of the ceremony. And, most importantly, he can provide calm and comforting support for you and your fiance.

Be sure you understand the laws governing a religious wedding ceremony. Some faiths do not allow marriages to be performed on certain days or at certain times of day. Some faiths will not permit a wedding to be performed outside a house of worship. Some faiths require that the bride wear a veil during the ceremony, and some require participation by the best man, maid of honor or parents of the bride and groom. Your clergyman can advise you on these matters.

If you and your fiance are of different faiths, you might have to do some investigating to find an officiant and a place to be married. Some interfaith marriages are performed by clergymen from both the bride's and the groom's faiths. Some are civil ceremonies performed by a judge, justice of the peace, or even a ship captain. If you are planning an interfaith ceremony but still want the ambiance of a chapel wedding, look for a nondenominational chapel in your area. Colleges and universities are a good place to start.

After consulting your clergyman, you might want to enlist the services of a **bridal consultant**. A consultant will help you arrange the details of the reception. She is usually well-connected with people and businesses who provide services for weddings, such as caterers, party supply houses, photographers, stationers, florists, musicians and even calligraphers. Often, working through a consultant can give you better prices than working on your own. A consultant is also well-versed in wedding etiquette and protocol, which comes in quite handy in sticky situations.

Invest in a **guide to wedding etiquette**. You'll sometimes find yourself in unfamiliar territory when you're making wedding arrangements. For example: What's the proper wording for a wedding announcement? If the bride's parents are divorced, should they still stand together in wedding photographs? An etiquette guide will help you through awkward moments and ensure that you're following accepted social procedure.

PROFESSIONAL ADVICE

You are about to enter the world of wedding professionals – individuals and businesses that provide services for weddings. At the top of most lists is the caterer. Developing a good working relationship with your caterer is extremely important. When you choose a caterer, be sure he is someone who makes your feel comfortable and confident. Basically, your wedding reception is in his hands.

The caterer, of course, provides the food for your wedding reception, but he can also be a very valuable resource for your overall wedding plan. Remember the caterer is a professional. He has organized and attended more weddings than anyone you're likely to meet (with the possible exception of your clergyman) and he can give you good advice on what works, what doesn't, and what will make your wedding a stunning success.

A wedding is a special occasion for the family and friends

Photography by Alan Khan and Christopher Poulos

Most of the time, the caterer will be on hand to supervise the table set-up and service for the reception. He may also act as a wedding director, overseeing the rehearsal and guiding the flow of the day.

When you meet with your caterer, ask a lot of questions. Be sure you understand the services he provides. Which services are standard (included in the flat fee) and which cost extra? Ask about table arrangement and size of tables. Carefully review the menu

selections. Discuss table linens, china and glassware. It's important that you know what to expect.

Your caterer can also recommend suppliers for your other wedding needs, such as florists, musicians and photographers. Sometimes a caterer will insist that you use a particular supplier. The choice is yours. Keep in mind, however, that if a caterer recommends a florist, for example, the two probably have a successful working relationship. This can help things run smoothly.

GENERAL RULES

We provide more information about musicians, photographers and florists throughout this book. Here are some general tips to keep in mind when dealing with suppliers:

❖ Choose people with whom you feel comfortable. Feel confident that they understand what you want and are willing to give it to you. Your supplier should be flexible and amenable to your wishes.

❖ Ask questions, and be sure you understand what you can expect from your suppliers. Watch out for hidden costs.

❖ Get it in writing. Don't rely on a verbal agreement. Read contracts carefully before signing.

❖ Don't be shy! You've probably never planned such a big and complicated event and you might feel a little shaky about making arrangements. Some suppliers (they are the exception!) will try to take advantage of your confusion. Stand firm and don't be bullied.

❖ Stay calm. There may be times in the coming months when you want to scream, or cry, or both! It will pass. Everthing will be wonderful. Remember that every bride is beautiful, and no wedding is ever as nice as your own.

BRIDAL
CALENDAR

Careful planning is the key to a happy and successful wedding day. If you decide on a formal wedding, begin preparations at least six months in advance (three months for an informal wedding). If you're planning for a June or October wedding (traditionally the most popular wedding months), begin contracting for locales and necessities as early as possible. Remember, although every wedding is different – it may be formal or informal, in a church, a registry office or in your backyard – it's important to plan every detail of your wedding. The following timetable will help.

FIRST DECISIONS FOR THE ENGAGED COUPLE

❖ Decide on the size and style of the wedding. Determine a date for the wedding, and have a back-up date in mind. Discuss your plans with the officiating clergyman or celebrant.

❖ Work out a budget.

❖ Compile a guest list in consultation with both families.

❖ Select and reserve a ceremony site and a reception location.

❖ Begin interviewing caterers, musicians, florists and photographers. Contact the best for your wedding.

❖ Choose your attendants: best man, maid or matron of honor, bridesmaids, ushers, flower girl and ring bearer.

❖ Consider styles for the bridal gown and veil, and bridesmaids' dresses. If you are making them yourself or having them made, choose patterns and fabrics, and arrange fittings. If you are ordering dresses from a bridal salon, start shopping as early as possible. It may take months for your gown to arrive.

❖ Decide on a color theme for the wedding.

❖ Plan the menswear and arrange for necessary rental.

❖ Think about your trousseau and going-away outfit.

❖ Select a honeymoon destination and make reservations.

❖ Select styles for stationery and invitations. If necessary, arrange for transportation to and from the wedding for yourself and/or bridal party.

❖ Arrange time off from work for your honeymoon.

Photographs are a lasting reminder of the wedding day

Photography by Alan Khan and Christopher Poulos

3 MONTHS TO GO

❖ Finalize the guest list.

❖ Order invitations and other stationery. If possible, pick up envelopes in advance and begin addressing them. Buy stamps.

❖ Choose wedding rings.

❖ For an at-home wedding arrange rental of a tent, chairs, cutlery and china, if necessary.

❖ Arrange to have your wedding cake made and decorated (it is considered bad luck to make your own).

❖ Confirm arrangements with the clergy or celebrant. Discuss the form of service you will have, church fees and music. Many religions recommend pre-marital counseling with clergy or support groups.

❖ With the caterer, organize menus for the wedding reception.

❖ Register with a store bridal registry.

❖ Book a hotel room for the night, if you are not leaving on your honeymoon until the following day. If you will have many guests from out of town, reserve a block of rooms at a nearby hotel, so your guests will have a place to stay. You do not have to pay for the rooms, simply reserve them.

❖ Finalize honeymoon plans. Apply for passports and visas. If you plan to change your name, allow plenty of time for new documents, such as passports and cheque books, to be issued.

❖ Decide on gifts for the bridal party.

2 MONTHS TO GO

❖ Mail wedding invitations. Record acceptances as they are received.

❖ Make a list of all wedding gifts received and send thank-you notes immediately.

❖ Organize wedding ceremony rehearsals with the clergy or celebrant and bridal party.

❖ Arrange with your hairstylist, manicurist and beautician for an appointment on the day or day before the wedding. It's a good idea to have a practice make-up and hairstyle session with your headpiece on.

❖ Apply for a marriage license.

❖ Visit your doctor for necessary blood tests and physical exams.

❖ Schedule a gown fitting.

1 MONTH TO GO

❖ Follow up with guests who haven't replied to the invitations and finalize guest list.

❖ Write place cards for the reception.

❖ Finalize the menus and beverage lists; arrange seating plan for the reception.

❖ Check that all bridal clothes, whether being made or rented, will be ready.

❖ Check that your trousseau is complete.

❖ If you plan to have a wedding portrait taken in advance, do it now.

❖ Prepare a newspaper announcement, if you wish; most newspapers provide forms for you to fill in.

❖ Insure wedding gifts, and amend your present policies to include joint coverage.

❖ Give a bridesmaid's lunch or dinner.

❖ Final gown fitting.

1 WEEK TO GO

❖ Pack for honeymoon.

❖ Hold final rehearsal for the ceremony and rehearsal dinner.

❖ Break in your wedding shoes at home.

❖ Arrange the bachelor party for at least one week before the wedding. The bride's night out with her girlfriends could be held the same evening.

❖ If you will change your name, begin contacting credit card companies, banks, Social Security, etc. for new cards or accounts.

ON THE DAY

❖ Attend to all your beauty preparations, then relax and enjoy yourself.

AFTERWARD

❖ Things must also be arranged for after the wedding. Ask someone to collect your gown and the groom's suit when you have changed into your going-away outfits. If you're leaving for your honeymoon immediately, be sure someone returns the groom's rented tuxedo!

❖ Wedding presents should be packed away and taken to your home if they were displayed at the reception.

BRIDAL BUDGET

A lovely affair need not be costly

❖ Items borrowed or rented must be returned promptly.

❖ Write thank-you notes after you return from your honeymoon.

A wedding is a celebration of love, and is a touching and exciting event whether it is simple or lavish. Don't be pushed into over-committing yourselves financially. With flair and imagination, costs can be kept to a minimum without losing any of the fun and meaning of the occasion. Organizing a wedding can place great strain on available resources, but customs are changing and the costs need no longer be met by the bride's parents alone. Early discussions about who should pay what expenses will help you decide how much to spend in which areas. The most important ingredients are free: planning, consideration and imagination.

Once you know your budget, work out your priorities and then work with your caterer, florist, photographer, travel agent and stationer to get the items and services you want at reasonable costs. Reserve at least 20 percent of the total budget to cover unforeseen expenses.

WHO PAYS FOR WHAT?

The following is a **traditional** breakdown of expenses. Attendants pay for their own transportation expenses into town for the wedding, their attire, wedding gifts and the bridal shower or bachelor party. The groom and his family pay for the bride's engagement and wedding rings, celebrant or church fees, gifts for the groom's attendants, flowers for the bridal party, the bride's wedding gift, accommodation for the groom's attendants if necessary and the honeymoon. The bride and her family pay for the invitations and announcements, engagement party, flowers for the ceremony and reception, groom's wedding gift and wedding ring, gifts for the bride's attendants, bridal outfit, accessories and trousseau, all ceremony fees except the celebrant, all photography, accommodation for bridesmaids, transportation for the wedding party and reception expenses. See the chart opposite.

Drawing up a guest list calls for good sense and tact. Both families should write a list of names of friends and family they would like to invite. If the number of guests grows too large for the church or for the budget, a tactful way to include everyone in the celebration is to have a large informal engagement party for all, and then a smaller wedding, with only immediate family and very close friends.

The style of wedding will certainly affect the costs. Most formal weddings are held in a church, with abundant flowers and decorations and there may be a soloist or choir as well as the traditional organist.

A semi-formal wedding can be held at almost any time of the day with any number of people present. The bridal party is often smaller than for a more formal occasion. A maid or matron of honor and best man may be the only attendants. A general rule for receptions is that the more formal the occasion, the more expensive it is. If you have an early morning wedding, a breakfast/brunch can be served either at home or in the garden; for a mid-morning wedding, the only essentials are cake and champagne; for a noon wedding, a light lunch is usually served and an early to mid-afternoon ceremony could be followed by a cold buffet. Late-afternoon ceremonies, however, are usually followed by a cocktail party and dinner, either seated or buffet-style, and dancing.

Don't forget to budget for your honeymoon. Include it in your initial wedding budget. It can be the vacation of your dreams if you take the time to plan carefully. Decide on your destination, the type of accommodation that appeals to you and how you want to travel. Other expenses to bear in mind are food and drinks, entertainment, tips, gifts, mementos and impulse spending, plus spare cash for emergencies.

Our honeymoon checklist below will help you to make all those important decisions. Use it as a guideline before you visit your travel agent.

HONEYMOON CHECKLIST
Decide on:
- ☐ destination
- ☐ type of travel
- ☐ type of accommodation: hotel/motel or self-contained apartment
- ☐ food and drinks
- ☐ entertainment
- ☐ car rental
- ☐ gifts
- ☐ mementos
- ☐ impulse spending
- ☐ spare cash for emergencies

WHO PAYS FOR WHAT?

BRIDE AND FAMILY	BRIDEGROOM AND FAMILY	ATTENDANTS
invitations	marriage license	bridal shower
engagement party	rehearsal dinner	bachelor party
flowers for ceremony and reception	flowers for bridal party	
groom's wedding gift and wedding ring	bride's wedding gift and wedding ring	
gifts for bride's attendants	gifts for groom's attendants	wedding present
bridal outfit, accessories and trousseau	own outfit	own outfit
ceremony fees (except for celebrant)	celebrant or church fees	
photography		
accommodation for bridesmaids (if necessary)	accommodation for groom's attendants (if necessary)	
transportation for wedding party to ceremony and reception	transportation for groom and best man to ceremony	transportation to wedding
reception expenses	honeymoon	

CHAMPAGNE BREAKFAST

The happy couple get off to a delicious start with a wedding breakfast. Or use these recipes as brunch for a bridal shower. Tangy Tomato Cooler, Berry Cornucopia and Grapefruit Compote add color to the happy occasion.

Back, from left: Strawberry Punch, Tangy Tomato Cooler, Fresh Berry Cornucopia, Grapefruit Compote Cups; center from left: Marmalade Muffins, Dill Pancakes with Oysters and Caviar, Potato and Sausage Frittata, Tomato and Spinach Roulade; front, from left: Cheese Pastry Cups with Salmon Souffle, Plain Crepes with mascarpone cheese and honey, Spinach Crepes with smoked salmon and avocado.

❖
GRAPEFRUIT COMPOTE CUPS

As a timesaver, prepare these the day before and store in the refrigerator. Take them out two hours before serving and allow them to return to room temperature.

Makes 10 servings.

- ☐ 1³/₄ cups dried apricots
- ☐ 1¹/₄ cups pitted prunes
- ☐ 2 cups dried apples
- ☐ ³/₄ cup dried peaches
- ☐ ³/₄ cup raisins
- ☐ 1³/₄ cups orange juice
- ☐ 1 cup water
- ☐ ¹/₂ cup sweet sherry
- ☐ 2 to 3 tablespoons honey
- ☐ 2 teaspoons chopped preserved ginger in syrup (or use crystallized)
- ☐ 5 medium grapefruit

1   Combine apricots, prunes, apples, peaches and raisins in a medium-size saucepan. Add orange juice, water, sherry, honey and ginger and bring to a boil over medium high heat, stirring to dissolve honey. Reduce heat to medium and cook 15 to 20 minutes or until fruit is tender.

2   Meanwhile, cut grapefruit in half crosswise. Using a grapefruite knife or small paring knife, section and remove as much of the fruit as possible leaving cups intact and reserving the extra fruit. Stack the empty cups together, place in a plastic bag, seal and refrigerate.

3   Remove fruit mixture from the heat and stir in grapefruit sections. Cool to room temperature. Cover and refrigerate.

4   When ready to serve spoon equal amounts of the fruit and syrup into the empty grapefruit cups.

❖
POTATO AND KIELBASA FRITTATA

The frittata can be partially prepared the night before, covered, refrigerated and baked just before serving. A non-stick pie plate is ideal for this dish.

Makes 10 servings.

- ☐ 1 tablespoon olive oil
- ☐ 1 large baking potato, pared and thinly sliced
- ☐ ¹/₄ pound Kielbasa (Polish sausage), sliced (¹/₂ cup)
- ☐ 1 small sweet red pepper, halved, cored, seeded and sliced into thin strips
- ☐ 4 green onions, finely chopped
- ☐ 6 eggs
- ☐ 2 tablespoons finely chopped fresh basil
- ☐ ¹/₂ teaspoon salt
- ☐ ¹/₈ to ¹/₄ teaspoon freshly ground black pepper
- ☐ ¹/₄ cup shredded Monteray Jack cheese

1   Preheat the oven to moderate (350°).
2   Brush a 9-inch pie plate with oil. Arrange the potato in a slightly overlapping circle on the prepared plate. Cover.
3   Bake in the preheated moderate oven (350°) for 30 minutes or until the potatoes are tender.
4   Arrange the slices of Kielbasa and pepper strips over the top of potatoes. Sprinkle with the onions.
5   Combine the eggs, basil, salt and pepper in a medium-size bowl; beat slightly.
6   Pour eggs over top of Kielbasa and vegetables. Sprinkle with cheese.
7   Return to the preheated moderate oven (350°) and bake for 15 to 20 minutes or until the eggs are set and the cheese is melted. Cool for 10 minutes before serving.

❖ MARMALADE MUFFINS ❖

These muffins keep very well, so they can be made one or two days in advance. Reheated in the microwave, six muffins at full power take 1¹/₂ to 2 minutes .

Makes 12 muffins.

- ☐ **2 cups sifted self-rising flour**
- ☐ **1 cup brown sugar, firmly packed**
- ☐ **2 teaspoons baking powder**
- ☐ **2 teaspoons ground allspice**
- ☐ **2 cups high fiber bran cereal**
- ☐ **1¹/₂ cups milk**
- ☐ **2 eggs**
- ☐ **¹/₂ cup (1 stick) butter or margarine, melted**
- ☐ **¹/₄ cup orange marmalade**

1   Preheat oven to hot (400°). Grease 12 muffin-pan cups.

2   Combine flour, brown sugar, baking powder and allspice on a sheet of waxed paper; set aside.

3   Place bran cereal and milk in a large bowl, stir together just until the milk is absorbed. Beat the eggs slightly in a small bowl and mix in the melted butter. Add to the cereal mixture, stirring until well combined. Stir in the dry ingredients, all at once just until moistened; do not overmix.

4   Spoon half of the batter equally into the prepared muffin-pan cups. Top with a level measuring teaspoon of marmalade. Cover each with an equal amount of the remaining batter.

5   Bake in the preheated hot oven (400°) for 20 to 25 minutes or until a wooden pick inserted in the centers comes out clean. Remove the pan to a wire rack. Loosen the muffins with a thin metal spatula and remove from the pan at once to prevent steaming.

❖ TOMATO AND SPINACH ❖ ROULADE

The filling can be made the day before. Cover the sauce with plastic food wrap and store in the refrigerator. Gently reheat the filling before spreading it on the roulade.

Makes 10 servings.

SPINACH FILLING
- ☐ **2 tablespoon butter or margarine**
- ☐ **1 medium onion, finely chopped (¹/₂ cup)**
- ☐ **8 spinach leaves, stems removed, washed and drained thoroughly and chopped**
- ☐ **1 cup ricotta cheese**
- ☐ **3 tablespoons toasted pine nuts**
- ☐ **1 teaspoon salt**
- ☐ **freshly ground black pepper**

TOMATO ROULADE
- ☐ **4 tablespoons butter or margarine**
- ☐ **¹/₂ cup unsifted all-purpose flour**
- ☐ **2 tablespoons chopped fresh basil**
- ☐ **¹/₂ cup milk**
- ☐ **¹/₂ cup sour cream**
- ☐ **4 eggs, separated**
- ☐ **2 tablespoons tomato paste**
- ☐ **grated Parmesan cheese**

1   To make Tomato Roulade: Preheat the oven to very hot (475°). Grease a 15 x 10 x 1-inch baking pan. Line the bottom with waxed paper; lightly grease the paper.

2   Melt the butter in a medium-size saucepan over medium-low heat. Stir in flour and basil. Cook, stirring constantly for 1-2 minutes. Combine the milk and sour cream and gradually add to the flour mixture, stirring or whisking constantly until the mixture thickens and bubbles. Continue stirring for 2 to 3 minutes or more.

3   Beat the egg yolks slightly in a medium-size bowl. Slowly stir in about ¹/₃ cup of the hot milk mixture; stir back into the saucepan. Cook over low heat, stirring constantly for 2 minutes. Remove from the heat. Stir in the tomato paste.

4   Beat the egg whites in a medium-size bowl until stiff but not dry peaks form. Gently fold the egg whites into the tomato mixture until no streaks of white remain.

Marmalade Muffins, Plain and Spinach Crepes with sweet and savory fillings, Tomato and Spinach Roulade

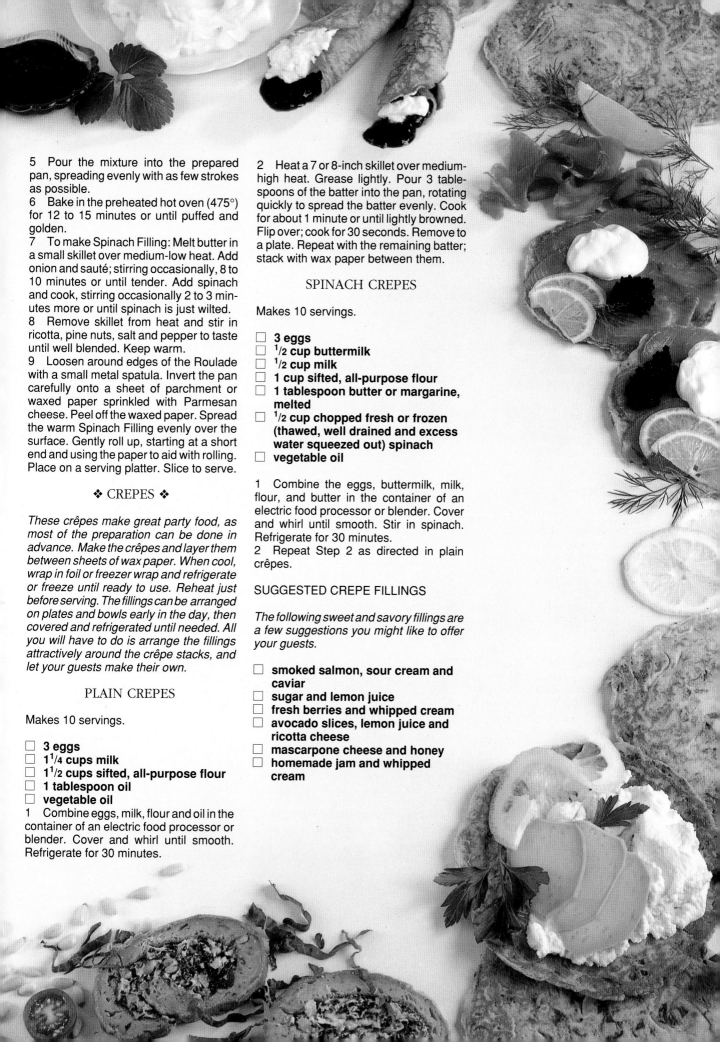

5 Pour the mixture into the prepared pan, spreading evenly with as few strokes as possible.

6 Bake in the preheated hot oven (475°) for 12 to 15 minutes or until puffed and golden.

7 To make Spinach Filling: Melt butter in a small skillet over medium-low heat. Add onion and sauté; stirring occasionally, 8 to 10 minutes or until tender. Add spinach and cook, stirring occasionally 2 to 3 minutes more or until spinach is just wilted.

8 Remove skillet from heat and stir in ricotta, pine nuts, salt and pepper to taste until well blended. Keep warm.

9 Loosen around edges of the Roulade with a small metal spatula. Invert the pan carefully onto a sheet of parchment or waxed paper sprinkled with Parmesan cheese. Peel off the waxed paper. Spread the warm Spinach Filling evenly over the surface. Gently roll up, starting at a short end and using the paper to aid with rolling. Place on a serving platter. Slice to serve.

❖ CREPES ❖

These crêpes make great party food, as most of the preparation can be done in advance. Make the crêpes and layer them between sheets of wax paper. When cool, wrap in foil or freezer wrap and refrigerate or freeze until ready to use. Reheat just before serving. The fillings can be arranged on plates and bowls early in the day, then covered and refrigerated until needed. All you will have to do is arrange the fillings attractively around the crêpe stacks, and let your guests make their own.

PLAIN CREPES

Makes 10 servings.

- [ ] **3 eggs**
- [ ] **1¼ cups milk**
- [ ] **1½ cups sifted, all-purpose flour**
- [ ] **1 tablespoon oil**
- [ ] **vegetable oil**

1 Combine eggs, milk, flour and oil in the container of an electric food processor or blender. Cover and whirl until smooth. Refrigerate for 30 minutes.

2 Heat a 7 or 8-inch skillet over medium-high heat. Grease lightly. Pour 3 tablespoons of the batter into the pan, rotating quickly to spread the batter evenly. Cook for about 1 minute or until lightly browned. Flip over; cook for 30 seconds. Remove to a plate. Repeat with the remaining batter; stack with wax paper between them.

SPINACH CREPES

Makes 10 servings.

- [ ] **3 eggs**
- [ ] **½ cup buttermilk**
- [ ] **½ cup milk**
- [ ] **1 cup sifted, all-purpose flour**
- [ ] **1 tablespoon butter or margarine, melted**
- [ ] **½ cup chopped fresh or frozen (thawed, well drained and excess water squeezed out) spinach**
- [ ] **vegetable oil**

1 Combine the eggs, buttermilk, milk, flour, and butter in the container of an electric food processor or blender. Cover and whirl until smooth. Stir in spinach. Refrigerate for 30 minutes.

2 Repeat Step 2 as directed in plain crêpes.

SUGGESTED CREPE FILLINGS

The following sweet and savory fillings are a few suggestions you might like to offer your guests.

- [ ] **smoked salmon, sour cream and caviar**
- [ ] **sugar and lemon juice**
- [ ] **fresh berries and whipped cream**
- [ ] **avocado slices, lemon juice and ricotta cheese**
- [ ] **mascarpone cheese and honey**
- [ ] **homemade jam and whipped cream**

❖ CHEESE PASTRY CUPS ❖
WITH SALMON SOUFFLE

Make the pastry cups in advance. They will keep in an airtight container for a week or can be frozen for up to one month.

Bake pastry cups at 425° for 10 minutes; then bake filled cups at 350° for 20 minutes.
Makes 12 servings.

CHEESE PASTRY
- ☐ **2 cups unsifted all-purpose flour**
- ☐ **6 tablespoons vegetable shortening**
- ☐ **6 tablespoons unsalted butter or margarine, cut into $1/2$-inch slices**
- ☐ **$2^1/2$ tablespoons grated Parmesan cheese**
- ☐ **2 tablespoons finely shredded Cheddar cheese**
- ☐ **2 to 3 tablespoons cold water**
- ☐ **1 tablespoon sour cream**
- ☐ **raw beans or rice (see Step 3)**

SOUFFLE FILLING
- ☐ **1 tablespoon butter or margarine**
- ☐ **1 tablespoon all-purpose flour**
- ☐ **$1/8$ teaspoon chili powder**
- ☐ **2-3 drops liquid red pepper seasoning**
- ☐ **1 can ($6^1/2$ to $7^1/2$ ounces) red salmon, drained and liquid reserved**
- ☐ **$1/2$ cup milk**
- ☐ **1 tablespoon mayonnaise**
- ☐ **1 tablespoon heavy cream**
- ☐ **$1/2$ teaspoon lemon juice**
- ☐ **2 eggs separated**

1 To make Cheese Pastry: Place flour in a large bowl. Cut in half of the shortening and half of the butter with a pastry blender or 2 knives until the mixture resembles fine breadcrumbs. Cut in the remaining shortening and remaining butter until the largest pieces are the size of peas. Stir in Parmesan and Cheddar cheeses.
2 Combine sour cream and water in a small bowl; mix together until well blended. Gradually add to the dry indredients, stirring with a fork, until the dough leaves the sides of the bowl clean and can be gathered into a ball. Wrap the ball of dough in plastic wrap. Refrigerate for at least 30 minutes before rolling.
3 Divide pastry into 10 portions. Keep all the portions wrapped in plastic wrap and refrigerated, except the one that is to be rolled. Roll out one portion of pastry on a lightly floured board or cloth to a round 1-inch larger that the diameter of a small tartlet pan measuring $3^1/2$-inches across the top. Fit round in tartlet pan. Prick holes all over the rounds with a fork and trim edges even with the pan. Line the pan with aluminum foil and fill with raw beans or rice. (This process, called "baking blind" prevents the dough from shrinking during

baking. Repeat with the remaining pastry.
4 Meanwhile, preheat the oven to hot (425°).
5 Place all 10 cups on a large baking sheet or on a $15^1/2$ x $10^1/2$ x 1-inch baking pan and bake in the preheated hot oven (425°) for 5 minutes, or until dough is set. Remove the foil and the beans or rice. Continue baking the pastry shells for 5 minutes more, or until the dough is golden. Remove the pastry cups from the oven to a wire rack to cool for 5 minutes. Carefully remove from pans, using a thin metal skewer to free stubborn spots (making sure not to pierce the crust). Return to wire rack to cool completely before filling.
6 Reduce oven temperature to moderate (350°).
7 To make Souffle Filling: Melt the butter in a medium-size saucepan over medium-low heat. Stir in flour, chili powder and liquid red pepper seasoning. Cook, stirring constantly for 1 to 2 minutes. Combine the reserved salmon liquid and milk and gradually add to the flour mixture, stirring or whisking constantly until the mixture thickens and bubbles. Continue stirring for 2 to 3 minutes more. Reduce heat to low.
8 Beat the egg yolks slightly in a medium-size bowl. Slowly stir in about $1/3$ cup of the hot milk mixture; stir back into the saucepan. Cook over low heat, stirring constantly, for 2 minutes. Remove from the heat. Stir in the salmon, mayonnaise, cream and lemon juice.
9 Beat the egg whites in a medium-size bowl until stiff but not dry peaks form. Gently fold the egg whites into the salmon mixture until no streaks of white remain.
10 Spoon equal amounts of the salmon mixture into each pastry cup. Place on a

large baking sheet or $15^1/2$ x $10^1/2$ x 1-inch baking pan.
11 Bake in the preheated moderate oven (350°) for 20 to 25 minutes, or until puffed and golden. Remove to a wire rack to cool slightly. Serve immediately.

❖ MINIATURE DILL PANCAKES
WITH OYSTERS AND CAVIAR ❖

Prepare pancakes in advance and freeze. Thaw and gently reheat when ready to serve.

Makes 25 servings.

PANCAKES
- ☐ **1 cup sifted, all-purpose flour**
- ☐ **2 teaspoons chopped fresh dill**
- ☐ **$1/4$ teaspoon baking soda**
- ☐ **$1/8$ teaspoon freshly ground black pepper**
- ☐ **1 egg**
- ☐ **1 cup buttermilk**
- ☐ **$1^1/2$ teaspoons butter or margarine, melted**
- ☐ **2 to 3 tablespoons butter or margarine, softened**
- ☐ **25 shelled oysters**
- ☐ **$1^1/2$ cups sour cream**
- ☐ **$1/2$ cup caviar or fish roe**
- ☐ **dill sprigs (optional)**
- ☐ **lemon slices (optional)**

1 Combine flour, dill, baking soda, black pepper, egg, buttermilk and melted butter in the container of an electric food processor or blender. Whirl at high speed until smooth.
2 Heat a heavy griddle or large skillet over medium heat; brush with the softened butter. Drop the batter, 1 to 2 tablespoonsful per pancake onto the griddle. When bubbles begin to appear on the surface and burst, turn the pancakes over and cook the other side until golden. Remove to a plate and keep warm.
3 Just before serving, top each pancake with an oyster and a spoonful of sour cream. Sprinkle each with about 1 teaspoonful of caviar. Garnish with dill and lemon slices, if you wish.

WEDDING FARE WITH FLAIR

WEDDING TIME	SUGGESTED MENU
early morning	breakfast or brunch served indoors or in the garden
mid-morning	cake and champagne
noon wedding	light lunch
early to mid-afternoon	cold buffet
late afternoon to evening	cocktail party dinner and dance

❖ TASTY TOPPINGS ❖
Try topping our dill pancakes with smoked salmon and mayonnaise, turkey and cranberry sauce or grated carrot and orange.

❖ TANGY TOMATO COOLER ❖

This is a real refresher without alcohol.

Makes 10 servings.

- ☐ **2 quarts tomato juice**
- ☐ **³/₄ cup lemon juice**
- ☐ **3 teaspoons Worcestershire sauce**
- ☐ **1¹/₂ teaspoons celery salt**
- ☐ **1 teaspoon grated lemon zest (yellow part of rind only)**
- ☐ **¹/₄ teaspoon chili powder**
- ☐ **ice cubes**
- ☐ **celery sticks (optional)**
- ☐ **lemon slices (optional)**

1 Combine tomato juice, lemon juice, Worcestershire sauce, celery salt, lemon zest and chili powder in a 2¹/₂ to 3-quart pitcher. Stir well.

2 Stir well and pour over ice cubes in a glass. Garnish each glass with celery sticks and lemon slices.

❖ STRAWBERRY PUNCH ❖

Makes 10 servings.

- ☐ **1¹/₂ cups sugar**
- ☐ **2 cups water**
- ☐ **1 pint strawberries, capped**
- ☐ **2 bottles non-alcoholic sparkling white-wine, chilled**
- ☐ **¹/₂ cup mint leaves**

1 Combine sugar and water in a medium-size saucepan. Cook over medium heat, stirring constantly until sugar dissolves. Bring to a boil, reduce heat and simmer for 10 minutes. Add 1 cup of the strawberries and simmer for 5 minutes. Slice remaining strawberries and reserve. Remove from heat and set aside to cool.

2 Pour cooled strawberry mixture into the container of an electric processor or blender. Whirl at high speed until pureed. Pour into an 8-inch cake pan and freeze until firm.

3 Unmold the strawberry mixture and break into bite sized pieces. Place in a 3-quart punch bowl. Slowly pour in the wine and stir briefly. Float remaining sliced berries on top and sprinkle with mint leaves.

❖ FRESH BERRY ❖ CORNUCOPIA

Make the pastry cornucopia two or three days in advance and store in an airtight container.

Makes 12 servings.

- ☐ **1 package (17¹/₂ ounces) prepared puff pastry sheets**
- ☐ **1 egg, slightly beaten**
- ☐ **IOX (confectioners') sugar**
- ☐ **fresh blueberries, raspberries and stawberries**

1 Reheat the oven to hot (400°).

2 Prepare the Cornucopia: Cut a piece of heavy duty aluminium foil into a rectangle 22¹/₂ x 12-inches. Roll into a cone shape 12-inches long by 6 inches in diameter at the open end. Crumple parchment or waxed paper and pack into the foil cone to help retain shape.

3 Roll pastry into a 24 x 10-inch rectangle. Cut off an 8-inch piece and cut into strips measuring 10 x ¹/₂-inches. Place strips ¹/₂-inch apart on a foiled lined cookie sheet. Cut remaining pastry into strips measuring 16 x ¹/₂-inches and weave across the 10 x ¹/₂-inch strips. Cover pastry with plastic wrap and chill for 15 minutes.

4 Remove plastic wrap and place foil mold diagonally across the pastry lattice, with open end pointing towards bottom left-hand corner of pastry. Gently fold top left-hand corner of pastry over foil mold towards bottom right-hand corner. Continue to roll mold towards bottom right-hand corner. Trim any loose pastry ends with a sharp knife. With remaining strips of pastry, weave a braid to fit around the opening of the cornucopia. Brush opening lightly with egg and fit braid around the entire opening, pressing gently to seal. Refrigerate for 15 minutes.

5 Brush the entire cornucopia with the egg and transfer to a large greased cookie sheet. Bake in the preheated hot oven (400°) for 20 to 25 minutes, or until golden brown. Cool completely on a wire rack. When completely cooled, remove foil and crumpled paper.

6 To serve: Dust with IOX (confectioners' powdered) sugar and fill with mixed berries.

WEDDING BELLES

Choosing her wedding gown is every bride's greatest pleasure and, at the same time, her greatest challenge. Use our guidelines to make the right choice.

There is a perfect dress style for every kind of figure. Once you've analyzed your shape, the next step is to select a design and fabric which best suits you. The type of gown you wear also depends on the type of ceremony you plan to have, the season, your personality and, of course, your budget. For an informal wedding, the bride may wear a dress that is long or grazes the calf; a veil or headpiece is optional. Add a splash of color by threading ribbon through your hair or adding colorful flowers to your bouquet. Semiformal wedding gowns are usually floor-length and a fingertip veil is worn. For a formal wedding, romance and ritual is everything – the more opulent and fanciful the dress, the better. Traditionally, a formal wedding was an all-white affair, but brides now also wear ivory, and gloves and train are optional. Attendants wear formal dress.

Overtrimming a gown is a common mistake. If you are overweight, lots of ruffles and bows can make you look even bigger, and if you are petite they can overwhelm you. Brides with broad hips should choose a gown with a skirt cut on the bias, to highlight more slender parts of the body such as the neck, arms or ankles.

Full-skirted styles are best suited to tall, slender figures

Brides who are tall with full figures should choose simple, tailored designs rather than bouffant or body-hugging gowns.

Once you have a good idea of the style that suits you best, arrange to have your gown made (if you don't intend to make it yourself), or rent or buy a gown. A good designer or salesperson will consider your features and your coloring and suggest ideas for the bouquet and accessories to complement the gown. State your budget to the designer or salesperson at the beginning. A great variety of styles are available in all price ranges, though fabrics may differ.

Clever use of fabric can transform a simple style

For brides who are short and full-figured, plain and simply styled gowns are best. Soft flowing skirts falling from a bodice with a simple neckline are also flattering.

Vertical lines and slim skirts create the illusion of extra height. Short, thin brides should avoid long trains, full sleeves, excessive trim and heavily textured fabrics.

If you are tall and thin, fullness is the key. You can achieve this by adding ruffles and bows, layering your fabric, or choosing a simple gown in a heavily textured fabric such as embossed satin, taffeta or lace. Full trains look wonderful and long sleeves disguise thin arms.

Slim-skirted styles give an impression of added height

Silk, organza, taffeta and lace are traditional favorites and always lovely.

Silk falls gracefully and lace looks rich and extravagant. Satin is sensuous and the luster will accentuate your curves. Organza is ideal for gowns of a bouffant style, and taffeta is a traditional favorite. If you are making your gown and plan to use lace with another fabric, buy the lace first as it is easier to match the fabric to the lace than the other way around.

If you decide to make your own gown, plan your sewing area carefully. Keep the floor immaculately clean; the area should be well lit with plenty of storage space. Keep an iron and ironing board close by. You'll

Pastel colors and floral prints are very popular for bridesmaids (above)

have to press down seams as you work. Never iron directly on your fabric. Place a damp cloth over the fabric before pressing to protect the delicate fibers and keep it clean.

Dresses for bridesmaids should complement the bride's. They are normally the same length as the bride's gown, but less elaborate in style and fabric. When choosing dresses for your attendants, select a color and style that will flatter each woman. Sometimes the simplest dresses are the most effective. Many brides prefer pastel shades for their attendants, but depending on the season, the style of dress and the fabric, a dark shade or print can be very beautiful.

❖ **THE SHOE BOX** ❖
Choose a simple style with a heel height appropriate to your size, your groom's height, and the style of your dress. White satin pumps or ballet slippers are traditional for brides and bridesmaids and may be dyed a darker shade after the wedding. Let your gown be your guide for choosing shoes. A sandal or even an ankle boot may be the perfect touch for you.

Beautiful ribbons, satin roses and delicate laces are the perfect trims for a wedding gown – don't forget finishing touches for your shoes!

BRIDAL REGISTRY

Compiling a list of gifts you and your husband-to-be would like to receive is not presumptuous. Most guests appreciate knowing what you want and need so they can buy "the perfect gift". The bridal registry can help you make sure you receive the household goods you need, in the styles and colors you like.

Department and specialty stores operate bridal registries at no cost to you. Through the registry, you make a list of the items available in the store that you would like to receive. When friends visit the store, they receive a copy of your list from which they may select a gift.

In addition to china, crystal and silver, you may register for sheets and towels, table linens, kitchen appliances, even luggage and camera equipment for your honeymoon! Cover as broad a range of items as possible to allow for your guests' budgets and tastes. Don't be afraid to list larger, more expensive items. Some guests may prefer to pool their resources to buy a more costly gift.

It is customary to register when your engagement is announced. The bride and groom should jointly decide on the items to include. Look through home decorating magazines for inspiration, go window shopping and consider all the rooms in your home and what you'll need to furnish them.

When you receive a gift, check to be sure it has arrived in good condition. If the item was damaged in transit, contact the store immediately for a replacement. You needn't inform the giver, unless she insured the package herself. Keep gifts in their original boxes in a secure place until you are ready to move them to your new home.

MUSICAL NOTES

Strike a joyous note for your wedding with carefully selected music.

When choosing music for the ceremony, begin by asking your clergyman about rules which may limit your selection. Some churches and synagogues include the services of an organist for the ceremony in their fees. If you prefer, hire a string quartet, flutist or vocalist for the occasion.

You can choose almost any type of music for the ceremony. Apart from hymns, there are many classical pieces which heighten the sense of occasion. Traditional ballads or folk music can be lovely. Ask the musicians for suggestions. Remember, contemporary music may be out of place at a formal wedding.

Some traditional favorites for the processional include Bach's "Jesu, Joy of Man's Desiring" and Schubert's "Ave Maria". Wagner's "Wedding March" from *Lohengrin* (we know it as "Here Comes the Bride") is the standard, but Mozart's *Allegro* or selections from Vivaldi's *Four Seasons* are also quite beautiful.

For the recessional march, the music should be lively. The usual choice is Mendelssohn's "Wedding March" from *A Midsummer Night's Dream*.

Music for the reception can range from a jazz pianist to a dance band, Latin music or even a disc jockey. Take your time when selecting musicians for the reception – a band can make or break the party. Booking agents provide tapes, and often videos, of their bands. If possible, go to hear the band perform in person.

Look for a band with a broad repertoire. Everyone loves to dance at weddings. Your band should play music that invites all the generations to take a turn on the dance floor.

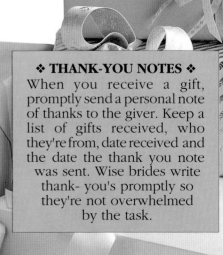

❖ **THANK-YOU NOTES** ❖
When you receive a gift, promptly send a personal note of thanks to the giver. Keep a list of gifts received, who they're from, date received and the date the thank you note was sent. Wise brides write thank-you's promptly so they're not overwhelmed by the task.

PEN TO PAPER

Make your invitations and thank-you notes as unique as your wedding. Hand-written invitations on handmade paper add a beautiful personal touch to the event.

The style of your invitations should reflect the formality of your wedding. Traditionally, invitations for a formal wedding are engraved or thermographed on white or ivory paper. Depending on the size of your wedding, you may prefer to invite some guests to the ceremony only. In this case, a separate invitation to the reception is usually printed on a matching card and enclosed only in the invitations for guests who will attend both the ceremony and the reception.

Some basic rules for wording are:
❖ When addressing the envelope, a guest's name and address should be written in full, no abbreviations.

In general, the only abbreviations used are "Mr", "Mrs", "Ms" and "Jr". All other forms of address, including Doctor, are written out.
❖ Dates are written in words, no numerals. For example, "Sunday, the fifth of June". You don't have to include the year.
❖ Times are spelled out. For example, five o'clock or half past three.
❖ If the invitation is for the wedding ceremony *and* reception, use the words "request the honour of your presence". The British spelling of honour (with a "u") is correct.
❖ If it is an invitation to the reception only, use the wording "request the pleasure of your

company".
❖ For a wedding at the reception site, write the name of the reception site only.
❖ While etiquette dictates that guests should respond to the invitation on their own, many invitations include response cards, often with stamped, self-addressed envelopes.
❖ The return address should be that of the bride's parents whenever possible.
For more information and tips for special cases, refer to a guide for wedding etiquette.

Some couples opt for a quiet family ceremony with a reception for all their friends and relatives afterward. Wording for this should be simple without any mention of the wedding locale. For close friends you wish to invite to the ceremony, enclose an informal handwritten note giving details of time and place.

There are lots of design ideas for invitations. Instead of engraving them, why not have the invitations written in calligraphy? Rather than gilt-edged cards, choose recycled paper which is available in colors and in different sized sheets; you can also buy envelopes to match.

Informal invitations are appropriate for weddings of 50 or fewer guests, a second marriage, a marriage between older people, or if the wedding has been arranged at short notice. Wording for these should be personalized and handwritten by the bride's mother or the bride herself.

❖ BRIDAL SHOWER ❖

One theory about the origin of the bridal shower may be traced back to old Holland. It is said that a young woman fell in love with a poor man and her father forbade the marriage, refusing to provide her dowry. Instead, the woman's friends "showered" her with gifts so that she would be able to marry and set up housekeeping with the man she loved. Traditionally, bridal showers have been a female-only affair, but it is not improper for the groom and his friends to attend if they choose. Stock-your-bar, barbeque or gardening showers are good ways to get the men involved.

❖ MAIL EARLY ❖

Order, or begin making your invitations as soon as your wedding date, venue and time have been confirmed. For a formal wedding, invitations should be mailed four to six weeks in advance. For an informal wedding, invitations may be mailed ten days in advance.

❖ A FLORAL TOUCH ❖

To decorate your notepaper with flowers, first press the flowers in a flower press or simply use sheets of blotting paper weighted down with heavy books. Then allow the flowers to dry until they feel papery to the touch. When the flowers are dry, glue them to the corners of your handmade notepaper.

Opposite and right: decorate old-fashioned-looking notepaper (available at larger stationery and wedding supply stores) with dried flowers, leaves and ribbons

JUST HEARD THE NEWS

When an engagement is announced, many folks like to send a small gift, along with their good wishes, to the bride. Here are some ideas for quick-to-craft essential household items to say "we wish you well."

❖ DAINTY TOWELS ❖

Easy: Achievable by anyone.

Make these beautiful towels for the bride's trousseau in a snap. Simply purchase a pair of towels or face cloths and stitch on some embroidered ribbon and lace in single or double rows for a truly special gift. Choose a trim with the same fiber content as the towels for easy laundering.

❖ MONOGRAMMED ❖ PILLOWCASES

Easy: Achievable by anyone.

MATERIALS (for each pair)
- ☐ **2¼ yds. of 44"-wide white pique or similar cotton**
- ☐ **⅞ yd. of 44"-wide printed cotton for borders**
- ☐ **about 4½ yds. single-fold bias tape**
- ☐ **dressmaker's carbon paper**
- ☐ **embroidery floss**

DIRECTIONS

1 *Cutting:* For each pillow case front, cut one white and one printed rectangle, each 21" x 30". Measure 4" from each edge of the print rectangle to draw a 4" border; cut on the drawn line. For the pillowcase back, cut a 21" x 36" white rectangle.

2 *Pillowcase Front:* Pin the right side of the print border to the wrong side of the matching white front; seam across one short end. Turn the border over, right side up. Press, then edgestitch the seam.

Turn under ⅜" at the inside border and press. (You'll have to clip the turnunder diagonally at each corner.) With the raw edges even, pin through both layers.

3 *Piping:* Fold the bias tape in half lengthwise and slide it under the inside border with its folded edge protruding as shown. Edgestitch the inner edge of the border through all thicknesses. Baste the three outside edges.

4 *Pillowcase Back:* Along one short end, turn under ¼", then ⅜" and stitch. Pin pillowcase back to pillowcase front with right sides together and three raw edges even. (The finished edge of the back will extend beyond the finished edge of front and become a hem. Now turn it over the front.) Stitch the pillowcase's three raw edges. Turn the case right side out.

4 *Monogram:* Through dressmaker's carbon paper, transfer a monogram (see page 23) to the white part of the pillowcase front. Embroider the letters in small continuous chain or back stitches.

❖ TRIMMED SHEETS ❖

Easy: Achievable by anyone.

MATERIALS
- ☐ **one white flat sheet**
- ☐ **strip of 5"-wide fabric, pieced as needed to measure 2" longer than the top edge of the sheet (see Note below).**
- ☐ **bias tape**

DIRECTIONS

Note: If you have to piece the fabric strip, take care to match print at each seam so the strip will appear to be continuous; press the seams open.

1 *Top Border:* Pin the contrast strip to the top edge of the sheet with the right side of the border against the wrong side of the sheet and the border extending beyond the sheet about an inch at each end. Stitch along the top edge and turn the border over to the right side of the sheet. Press. Turn under ⅜" at the long edge of the border and press.

2 *Piping:* Turn the bias tape in half lengthwise. Slide it under the pressed border edge and pin, so the tape's folded edge protrudes. Turn under the extra fabric at each end of the border, then edgestitch the long border edge through all layers. Seam each end of the border to match the side hems of the sheet, if there are any.

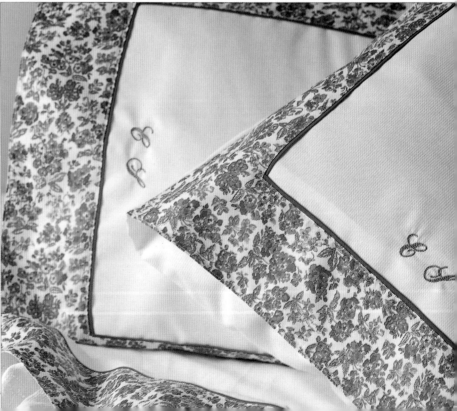

Above: Dainty Towels; right: Monogrammed Pillow Cases and Trimmed Sheet

PERSONAL
TOUCHES

A B C D E

F G H I J

K L M N

O P Q R

S T U V W

X Y Z

❖ PLACE MATS ❖

Average: For those with some experience in sewing.

These quilted and trimmed paisley place mats will grace the newlyweds' table. Make the napkins in the same fabric.

MATERIALS (for each mat)
- [ ] **⁷/₈ yd. of 44"-wide cotton print fabric**
- [ ] **14" x 20" piece of synthetic batting**
- [ ] **2 yds. single-fold bias tape**

DIRECTIONS

1 *Cutting:* Cut a mat front 14" x 20" and a mat back/border piece 22¹/₂" x 28¹/₂".

2 *Padding:* Baste batting to wrong side of mat front.

3 *Border:* Center the mat front on the wrong side of the mat back/border piece and baste it into place. Turn over ³/₈" on each edge of the large piece and press. Turn in each edge again, so it will lap ¹/₂" over the edges of the mat front. At each corner, pin the adjoining borders into a diagonal seam to make the miter. Cut away the extra fabric ¹/₂" above the pinned seam. Unpin each corner and re-pin it,

right sides together ¹/₂" from the mitered edges; stitch and press the seam open. Turn the corner right side out again.

4 *Piping:* Fold binding in half lengthwise and slide it under the turned-under border so its folded edge protrudes as shown. Edgestitch through all thicknesses.

❖ NAPKINS ❖

Average: For those with some experience in sewing.

Printed cotton napkins with attractively mitred corners complement the paisley place mats.

24

MATERIALS (for each napkin)
- [ ] **a 17$\frac{1}{2}$" square and four 3$\frac{3}{8}$" x 18" strips of fabric**
- [ ] **2 yds. of single-fold bias tape**

DIRECTIONS

1   *Frame:* Place two strips right sides together with edges even. Fold one short end over diagonally so it meets one long edge of the strip; press the fold. The diagonal fold will be the seamline. Stitch on the seamline, then trim off the excess fabric $\frac{1}{2}$" outside the seamline; press the seam open. You have made two adjoining sides of the frame. Add one strip at a time in the same way (and 3 seams) to complete the frame.

2   *Border:* Pin the right side of the frame against the wrong side of the square. Stitch $\frac{3}{8}$" from the edges. Turn the border over to the right side and press. Topstitch along each outside edge. Turn in $\frac{3}{8}$" along each inside edge of the border, clipping diagonally to each corner; press.

3   *Piping:* Fold the bias tape in half lengthwise and slide it under the pressed edge of border so its folded edge protrudes as shown. Edgestitch through all layers.

❖ CORK MATS ❖

Easy: Achievable by anyone.
A practical cork mat can become a very pretty one with a little paint and imagination. We painted our mats (photo page 24) with a motif from the place mat and napkin fabric using acrylic paints. If you are less confident of your artistic skills, try painting a simple geometric motif or flower outline.

❖ PADDED FLORAL HATBOX ❖

Average: For those with some experience in crafting.

MATERIALS
- [ ] **a round cardboard or balsa wood box**
- [ ] **cotton fabric**
- [ ] **synthetic batting**
- [ ] **craft glue**
- [ ] **tape measure**
- [ ] **masking tape**

DIRECTIONS

1   *Lid, Cutting:* Trace the lid top to the wrong side of fabric and cut out a circle $\frac{3}{4}$" *outside* the traced line. Cut the same circle from batting. Take a tape measure around the lid sides and add 1" to this circumference; then measure the depth of the lid inside *plus* outside and add 1". Cut a fabric rectangle to this length and depth.

2   *Lid, Assembly:* Center the batting circle over the lid top. Draw its edges down the lid sides and fasten it with short pieces of tape, cutting out the little wedges of extra fulness as needed. Repeat with the fabric circle. Turn under $\frac{1}{2}$" at each long edge and one short edge of the other lid piece and press. With the turned under edge at the top, wrap and glue it around the lid sides, inside and out, lapping the turned-under end over the opposite raw end.

3   *Box, Cutting:* Tracing the box bottom and measuring the box sides, cut out a fabric circle and rectangle in the same way as you did for the lid in Step 1. With the lid on, trace its lower edge to the box. Cut batting in a width to measure from this line to the box bottom and in a length to match the box's circumference.

4   *Box, Assembly:* Glue batting around the box from the penciled line to the bottom. Glue fabric circle to the box bottom as you did the lid top. Cover the box sides as you did the lid sides (see Step 2).

Opposite: Place Mats, Napkins, Hand-Painted Cork Mats.
Below: Floral Hat Boxes

FOR THE
FLOWER GIRL

The perfect gift for the flower girl is a charming white mouse, dressed just as she is! Remember to add the wreath of flowers around the mouse's ears.

❖ A WEDDING MOUSE ❖

If your flower girl is less than three years old, it would be wise to omit the pearl necklace and embroider the eyes.

MATERIALS
- [ ] **12" of 25"-wide felt**
- [ ] **2 small pearl beads or embroidery floss for eyes**
- [ ] **synthetic stuffing**
- [ ] **scraps of fabric (if possible, from the flower girl's dress)**
- [ ] **strung "pearls"**
- [ ] **buttontwist thread and white glue for whiskers**
- [ ] **¹/₈-inch-wide satin ribbon**

DIRECTIONS

1 *Enlarging the pattern:* Draw a series of vertical parallel lines 1" apart. At right angles to these, draw a series of horizontal lines 1" apart to complete the grid of 1" blocks. Now copy the pattern pieces from page 36 on to your own grid, imitating the solid lines, one block at a time. Label each piece and copy the notches. You don't need to copy seamlines; just take ¹/₄" seams.

2 *Tail:* Cut a strip of felt 1" x 6". Fold it in half lengthwise and stitch the raw edges together with small zigzag stitches, tapering to a point at one end. Trim off excess felt at the pointed end. Stuff the tail.

3 *Body:* Seam the pair of body pieces together, from the straight, bottom edge up to the head and down the back, stopping at the top notch near the bottom. Fold the base in half lengthwise and mark the centerline at each end of the fold. Stitch the base to the body, matching each center mark to a seam, and leave an opening for turning. Turn it right side out. Insert the blunt end of a tail between notches and close the seam by hand. Stuff the mouse and close the opening by hand.

A white felt mouse in her wedding outfit will delight the flower girl

4 *Feet:* Seam each pair of feet together except at the straight edge. Clip the seam allowance at both inside corners. Turn feet right side out and stuff them. Handsew through the straight edges with strong thread, pulling it up slightly, then sew that edge to the mouse between the two notches shown in the pattern.

5 *Face:* Sew a bead to the X at each side of the head, pulling up the threads to contour the face*. Draw buttontwist thread several times through the nose at the circle (see pattern) for whiskers and fix them in place with a dab of white glue.

*Or for young children, embroider the eyes with satin stitches.

6 *Ears:* Seam each pair of ears together except at the straight edge. Turn them right side out and stuff them lightly. Fold each corner to the center of the straight edge and stitch through all layers by hand with strong thread. Draw up the thread to gather slightly and sew the ears to the head behind the eyes (see photo).

7 *Arms:* Seam each pair of arms together, leaving an opening for turning. Turn and stuff; close opening by hand. At the top curve, handsew each arm to the body.

8 *Dress:* The mouse's dress is three ruffles (or two would do). The narrowest is at the neck and the widest at the hem. With pinking shears, if you have them, cut strips twice the finished width and twice the finished length desired. On each strip, seam the short ends right sides together and press the seam open. Turn it right side out and fold the resulting loop in half lengthwise, wrong sides facing; press. Sew a gathering row ¹/₄" from the raw edges; draw up the gathers to fit the mouse, fasten the thread ends and tack the ruffles to the mouse through the gathering stitches.

9 *Finishing (Optional):* Tie a fabric bow around her waist. Sew ribbon roses (see page 61) or artifical flowers over her head. Add a string of pearls if you like.

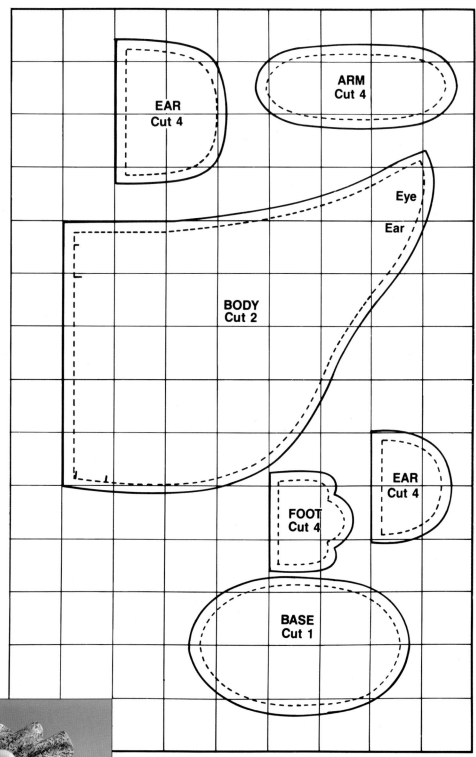

EAR
Cut 4

ARM
Cut 4

Eye

Ear

BODY
Cut 2

EAR
Cut 4

FOOT
Cut 4

BASE
Cut 1

Each square is 1 inch.

SHOWER BASKETS

A beautiful basket, trimmed and filled with pretty and practical items for the home, makes a wonderful shower gift. Choose a basket that will best suit the bride and groom, such as a kitchen basket for avid cooks or a garden basket for those with green thumbs.

❖ BATHROOM BASKET ❖

MATERIALS

- [ ] **a shallow cane basket with handle**
- [ ] **printed cotton fabric**
- [ ] **fusible interfacing**
- [ ] **strong thread for gathering**
- [ ] **bathroom accessories to fill the basket**
- [ ] **newspaper and tailor's chalk for pattern**
- [ ] **sewing thread to match fabric**

DIRECTIONS

1 *Liner pattern - Bottom* (without seam allowance): Draw a tape measure down and across the inside basket with one tape edge at the center of each handle. Chalk this centerline across the inside basket (down the sides and across the bottom). Set a piece of paper inside the basket. Holding it in place with one hand, mark on it the outline of the bottom with tailor's chalk, pressing against the crease where the basket sides begin. Also mark the centerline at each end of the pattern; cut out the paper pattern along the chalkline.

2 *Liner pattern - Sides* (without seam allowance): Place another piece of paper (large enough to cover the basket sides from top to bottom between two centerlines) against the inner side of half the basket. Smoothing out the extra fulness into darts over the basket bottom, chalk the edge of the basket bottom, then the top edge of the basket side. Fold each end of the paper along the centerline of one handle. Remove the paper and cut it out on both chalked edges and on the crease at each end.

3 *Cutting:* Cut a liner bottom from fabric, *1/2" ouside the paper pattern* and notch each end at the centerline. On folded fabric, cut a pair of liner sides, *1/2" outside each edge of the paper pattern.* Fuse interfacing to the wrong side of each of these three pieces. Measure around the top edge of the basket; cut two ruffle strips each of this length. Make their width twice the finished depth you want plus 1".

4 *Liner:* Seam the pair of liner sides together at the short ends; press the seams open. Then seam them to the liner bottom with a seam at each notch.

5 *Ruffles:* Turn in 1/2" at each short end and press. Then fold each ruffle strip in half lengthwise, wrong sides together. Using strong thread, sew gathering stitches 1/2" from the raw edges. Sew two more rows about 1/4" apart, further into the ruffle so they will fall just below the lip of the basket (see photo). With right sides together and raw edges even, pin a ruffle to each side of the liner from seam to seam; draw up the fulness to fit the liner and stitch. Place the liner in the basket, draw up the outer pair of gathering rows to fit the basket and tie off the thread ends.

6 *Handle:* Cut a strip of fabric twice the length of the handle and 1 1/2" wider than its girth. At each long edge, turn 3/8" to the wrong side and press. Fold the strip in half with wrong sides together and folded edges even. About 3/16" from the fold, sew a gathering row. From each open edge sew a gathering row about 3/16" from the pressed fold. Place the cover over the handle, with the folded edge at the top. Pull up its gathers to fit the handle and tie off the thread ends. Draw up both the bottom edges to fit and handsew them together through the gathering stitches. Handsew the ends of the cover to the liner.

7 *Bows:* Cut two 8'" x 32" strips for bows. Fold each in half lengthwise, right sides together. Cut the ends off at an angle. Stitch 3/8" from raw edges, leaving an

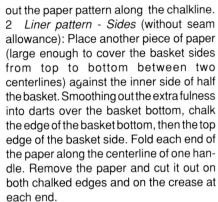

Left: Bathroom Basket filled with Dainty Towels, soaps, bath sponge and loofah

opening for turning. Turn right side out and press. Close opening by hand. Tie a bow at each end of the handle.

6   Fill the basket with bathroom goodies such as Dainty Towels (see page 22), loofah, soap, scented powder, or Floral Bath Oil (right).

❖ FLORAL BATH FRESHENER ❖

Make a bottle of delightful scented bath freshener and another of luxurious bath oil to include in your Bathroom Basket.

MATERIALS
- ☐ **1 pint of flower petals: rose, cornflower, violet, lavender, lilac, freesia or other scented flowers**
- ☐ **1 pint white wine vinegar**
- ☐ **$^1/_2$ pint water**
- ☐ **square of cheesecloth**
- ☐ **decorative bottle**

DIRECTIONS
1   Fill jars or bottles with rose, violet or other scented flower petals.
2   Mix vinegar and water and heat mixture until just boiling. Pour over flower petals in bottle.
3   Close bottle and leave in a warm spot for 3-4 weeks. Shake contents of bottle every day.
4   Strain contents through cheesecloth into a pretty bottle. If you wish, you can strengthen the scent by repeating the process using fresh flowers.

❖ FLORAL BATH OIL ❖

MATERIALS
- ☐ **6 ounces glycerine**
- ☐ **2 ounces floral oil of your choice, such as rose, lavender or violet**
- ☐ **decorative bottle**

DIRECTIONS
1   Whisk ingredients together until well mixed.
2   Pour into pretty bottle.
3   Label bottle with type of flower used and instruction to add one teaspoon to a hot bath.

❖ KITCHEN BASKET ❖

Fill a white wicker basket with useful kitchen utensils, a pretty tablecloth and matching napkins, a pair of cups and saucers and some delicious homemade preserves (see recipes on pages 30–31). To make the tablecloth, simply hem the edges of 1 yard square of cotton fabric and sew napkins to match, following the instructions on page 24. Trim the basket with a generous bow made from remnants of the tablecloth fabric.

❖ GARDEN BASKET ❖

This 'basket' is actually a wonderful terra-cotta pot filled to the brim with useful gifts for the gardener. Include such items as gloves, trowel, packets of seeds, potted plant decorations, clay herb markers, a sun hat and a gardener's apron.

❖ GARDENER'S APRON ❖

MATERIALS
- ☐ **$^3/_4$ yd. of sturdy fabric, such as sailcloth or denim**
- ☐ **two D-rings**

DIRECTIONS
1   *Cutting:* Cut one 4"-wide waistband, pieced as needed to go twice around your waist and to fasten with D-rings. Cut one 16" square for the pocket and two 12" x 16" rectangles for a lined apron.
2   *Pocket:* Fold pocket in half and pin it to one apron piece (right side up) with raw edges even and folded edge upward.
3   *Apron:* Place the second apron piece on top (over the pocket) with right sides together. Round off the two lower corners to match. Stitch $^3/_8$" from side and lower edges through all thicknesses. Turn apron right side out and press. Stitch down the center of the pocket, to make two.

Below: Kitchen Basket with mugs, spoons, preserves and napkins

Above: Garden Basket containing tools, gloves, and Gardeners Apron

4   *Waistband:* Turn in $^3/_8$" on each edge of the waistband and press. Fold it in half lengthwise. With center fronts matching, slide the apron between the pressed edges of the waistband and pin through all layers. Pin the remaining edges of the band together. Edgestitch around all four edges of the band, catching in the apron. Fold one end over the D-rings and stitch across the band securely to enclose them.

PANTRY TREATS

In a pickle deciding what to give the bride to stock her pantry? Homemade jam, chutney, and vinegar in attractive jars are a delectable solution.

❖ MIDSUMMER NIGHT'S JAM ❖

This jam can be made using any combination of berries, such as blackberries, blueberries, raspberries or strawberries.

Makes about three half-pint jars.
- [ ] $1/2$ to $1^3/4$ **pounds mixed berries**
- [ ] **4 cups sugar**
- [ ] **1 cup water**
- [ ] **juice of 1 lemon**

1 Wash 3 half-pint size canning jars, lids and bands in hot soapy water. Rinse. Leave the jars in hot water until needed. Place the lids and bands in a saucepan of simmering water until ready to use.
2 Combine berries, sugar, water and lemon juice in a large heavy saucepan and cook over low heat, stirring occasionally until the fruit softens and the sugar dissolves.
3 Increase the heat to medium-high; bring to a boil and boil, stirring occasionally for 20 to 25 minutes, or until temperature reaches 218° to 220° on a candy thermometer. Test, if jam is set by dropping a spoonful onto a chilled saucer and let it set at room temperature. The jam is set when the skin wrinkles if pushed. Remove from heat and let stand 1 to 2 minutes. Skim foam from surface.
4 Pour the jam into the clean, hot canning jars, using a wide-mouth funnel; leave a $1/4$-inch headspace. Run a long thin non-metallic spatula around the inside of the jar to release trapped air bubbles. Wipe the jar rims and threads clean with a damp cloth. Cover the jars with the hot lids; screw on the band firmly.
5 Process the jars in a boiling water bath for 5 minutes (the water should cover the jars by 1 to 2 inches). Remove the jars from the boiling water to a wire rack. Let stand for 12 hours. Test for seals. Label, date and store in a cool, dark place.

❖ HERB VINEGARS ❖

Use fresh herbs such as basil, tarragon, thyme or rosemary. For something different, use red or white wine vinegar.

Makes 1 quart.

- [ ] **2 cups fresh herbs**
- [ ] **1 quart (4 cups) vinegar**

1 Wash the herbs, gently shake and pat dry. Crush slightly.
2 Place desired herb in a clean, sterilized bottle and pour vinegar over herbs. Seal tightly and leave in a warm place such as a sunny windowsill for 3 to 4 weeks.
3 Strain the vinegar through several layers of cheesecloth into another sterilized bottle. Add a fresh herb sprig; seal and label.

❖ BEET, ORANGE ❖ AND APPLE CHUTNEY

Makes about 4 pint jars
- [ ] $2^1/4$ **pounds beets**
- [ ] **2 cups red wine vinegar**
- [ ] **1 cup sugar**
- [ ] **1 large onion, finely chopped (1 cup)**
- [ ] **1 teaspoon ground allspice**
- [ ] **2 large Granny Smith apples, peeled, cored and chopped**
- [ ] **1 orange**

1 Remove all but 1 inch of stem from the beets. Bring 4 cups of water to a boil in a large saucepan over hight heat. Add beets, return to a boil; reduce heat to medium; cover and boil 35 to 45 minutes or until tender. Drain, submerge in cold water 1 to 2 minutes, peel, remove stem or root ends and chop.
2 Meanwhile, wash 4-pint size canning jars, lids and bands in hot, soapy water. Rinse. Leave the jars in hot water until needed. Place the lids and bands in a saucepan of simmering water until ready to use.
3 Combine vinegar, sugar, onion, and allspice in a 5-quart Dutch oven or large saucepan. Bring to a boil over medium heat, stirring occasionally until the sugar dissolves. Add apple, reduce the heat to low and simmer for 15 minutes or until apple starts to break up. Stir in beets and orange and cook for 5 more minutes.
4 Pack the chutney into the clean, hot canning jars using a wide-mouth funnel; leave a $1/4$-inch headspace. Run a long

❖ PRESERVING TIPS ❖
When giving unusual preserves, tie an attractive label around the neck of the jar with serving suggestions. You might also like to include the recipe, on a label around the neck of the jar or written on pretty paper and placed in an envelope to go with the preserves. Decorate the jar with ribbon or a lacy doily gathered over the top of the jar.

thin nonmetallic spatula around the inside of the jars to release trapped air bubbles. Wipe the jar rims and threads clean with a damp cloth. Cover jars with the hot lids; screw on the bands firmly.

5   Process the jars in a boiling water bath for 30 minutes (the water should cover the jars by 1 to 2 inches). Remove the jars from the boiling water bath to a wire rack. Let stand for 12 hours. Test seals. Label, date and store in a cool, dark place.

❖ PICKLED PEPPERS ❖

Makes 1 quart jar.
- [ ] **2 large onions, sliced into ¼-inch rings (2 cups)**
- [ ] **2 large sweet green peppers, cored, seeded and sliced into ¼-inch rings**
- [ ] **2 large sweet red peppers, cored, seeded and sliced into ¼-inch rings**
- [ ] **2 large sweet yellow peppers, cored, seeded and sliced into ¼-inch rings**
- [ ] **2 tablespoons coarse (kosher)**

cooking salt
- [ ] **1½ cups white wine vinegar**
- [ ] **¾ cup sugar**
- [ ] **2 teaspoons black peppercorns**
- [ ] **1 teaspoon mustard seeds**
- [ ] **2 bay leaves**
- [ ] **1 red chili, seeded and finely chopped**

1   Combine onions, green, red and yellow peppers and salt in large nonmetallic bowl. Cover and let stand overnight.

2   Wash a quart size canning jar, lid and band in hot, soapy water. Rinse. Leave the jar in the hot water until needed. Place lid and band in a saucepan of simmering water until ready to use.

3   Drain and rinse vegetables under cold running water. Drain and pat dry with paper towelling.

4   Combine the vinegar, sugar, peppercorns and mustard seeds in a small saucepan. Bring to a boil over medium heat , stirring occasionally until the sugar dissolves. Reduce the heat to low and simmer, uncovered, for 3 minutes.

5   Using clean, sterilized tongs, pack the peppers, onion, bay leaves and red chili peppers firmly into the clean, hot canning jar; leaving a ¼-inch headspace. Make sure there is enough liquid to cover the vegetables; if necessary, add additional vinegar. Cover the jar with the hot lid; screw on the band firmly.

6   Process the jar in a boiling water bath for 10 minutes (the water should cover the jar by 1 to 2 inches). Remove the jar from the boiling water to a wire rack. Let stand for 12 hours. Test for seal. Label, date and store in a cool, dark place.

GENERAL DIRECTIONS FOR CANNING AND HOT WATER BATH PROCESS

Follow all the directions carefully and do not take any shortcuts.

1   Place the hot water bath canner on a surface burner. Add water to half-fill, cover the canner and bring the water to boiling while preparing the jars and food.

2   Wash the jars in hot sudsy water. Rinse well and leave in hot water.

3   Place new lids in a saucepan of simmering water.

4   Follow individual recipe directions.

5   Remove the jars from the water, one at a time; place on paper toweling or clean cloth. Pack and/or ladle the food into jars.

6   Wipe the tops and outside rims of the jars with a clean cloth. Place lids on top and screw rings on tightly, but do not use force.

7   Place the jars in the canner rack and lower into rapidly boiling water, adding additional boiling water if the level of water is not 2 inches above the jars. Cover canner and return to a full boil. Process following the time given in the individual recipe.

8   Remove the jars from the canner with tongs and place, at least 3 inches apart, on a wire rack or cloth-lined surface until cool.

9   Test all the jars, to be sure they are sealed, by tapping with a spoon. A clear ringing sound means a good seal. If the jars are not properly sealed, store in the refrigerator and plan to use within a month, or pour the contents of the jar into a bowl and process again from Step 5.

11   Remove the metal rings. Wipe the jars with a clean dampened cloth. Label, date and store the jars in a cool, dark, dry place.

Herb vinegar looks wonderful in an unusual bottle.

❖

SILKY SATIN HANGERS

Average: For those with some experience in sewing.

These two hangers are both made following the same instructions, one is trimmed with a satin bow, the other has a heart-shaped sachet attached to the hook.

MATERIALS
- ☐ **a wooden coat hanger**
- ☐ **two pieces of satin, each 3³/₄" x 40"**
- ☐ **synthetic batting**
- ☐ **¹/₁₆" wide satin ribbon**
- ☐ **1 yd. of gathered lace**
- ☐ **For heart sachet, a scrap of cardboard, tulle and satin; lavender or potpourri and white glue**

DIRECTIONS

1 *Batting:* Wrap batting around the hanger and sew it smoothly into place by hand. It should measure about 4" around in girth.

2 *Gathering:* At each edge of each satin strip, turn ¹/₂" to the wrong side and press. With the longest machine stitch, sew a gathering thread ¹/₄" from each edge.

3 *Top and Ends:* Pin the strips, wrong sides together, at one long and two short edges. Mark the center of the top edge. Draw up the top gathering, insert the hanger with the hook at the center mark and finish drawing up the gathers to fit the hanger. By hand, sew the two layers together through the gathering stitches at the top edge, then at each end, drawing up the gathers to fit the hanger.

4 *Bottom:* At the open edges, draw up the gathers to fit the hanger. Insert the gathered edge of the lace and pin. Through the gathering stitches, sew the edges together by hand, catching in the lace.

5 *Hook:* Thread a long-eyed needle with narrow satin ribbon and cover hook with buttonhole stitches from its tip to its base, then sew the lowest ribbon to the fabric cover.

6 *Sachet:* On cardboard, draw a symmetrical heart about 2¹/₂" long. Trace it once to the wrong side of satin and ³/₈" outside the drawn line; trace it again and cut on the drawn line. Center the cardboard heart on the wrong side of the large heart, turn the satin edges up over the cardboard and glue them in place, clipping out the fulness at the curved edges so the fabric will lie flat. Glue the smaller heart on top, right side up. Glue a tulle heart over that, leaving a small opening at the top. Push potpourri through the opening, then insert both ends of a 7" long ribbon for the hanger. Glue down the ribbon ends, then the open edge of tulle. Glue or sew gathered lace around the heart. Tie a ribbon bow and sew it to the heart. Hang the heart from the hook.

THE BRIDE

❖

EMBROIDERED LINGERIE BAG

Average: For those with some experience in sewing and embroidery.

Grub rose embroidered organza makes this glamorous bag for packing honeymoon "dainties".

MATERIALS
- ☐ **two pieces of organza, each 11" x 16"**
- ☐ **1 yd. ¼"- wide satin ribbon**
- ☐ **embroidery floss: green and shades of pink and yellow**

DIRECTIONS

1 *Buttonholes:* Bring the two 16" edges of the bag front together and fold the piece in half vertically; lightly press the top 5" of the fold. Mark two ½" vertical buttonholes, ¼" each side of the center crease, starting 4" below the top edge; work them by hand or machine.

2 *Embroidery:* Lightly draw the roses on each lower corner of the bag front, leaving at least two or three inches of space between the roses and the edges. Work the roses in bullion stitches; make chain stitch leaves and stemstitch stems (see page 37).

3 *French Seams:* Pin bag front to bag back, wrong sides together. Stitch ¼" from the side and bottom edges, curving both bottom corners(see photo). Trim the seam allowance to ⅛". Turn the bag wrong side out, i.e. with organza right sides together, and stitch ³⁄₁₆" seams to encase the raw edges. Turn the bag right side out and press.

4 *Casing:* At the top edge, turn under ¼", then 2¼" and pin the hem so it can be stitched just below the pair of buttonholes; stitch. Stitch again, just above the buttonholes, to make the casing. Thread ribbon through the casing. Tie a knot at each end of the ribbon.

THE RING PILLOW

*The best man won't have to worry about losing the ring
when it sits, tied with satin ribbon, on this beautiful pillow
carried down the aisle by a charming ring bearer.*

*This lovely ring pillow can be made for
one ring or two. After the wedding it may
be used as a throw pillow in the
bedroom, or tucked away for the next
wedding in the family*

❖ RING PILLOW ❖

Average: For those with some
experience in sewing.

MATERIALS
☐ ³/₄ yd. x 24"-wide silk voile for
   pillow back and front
☐ **11" square of silk satin for front**
   lining
☐ **10" square knife-edge pillow form**
☐ **2¹/₂ yds. of 2¹/₂"-wide lace for**
   ruffle
☐ **1¹/₄ yds. satin piping**
☐ **10" zipper**
☐ **1 yd. of ¹/₄"-wide satin ribbon**
☐ **1¹/₄ yds. 2¹/₄"-wide insertion lace**

DIRECTIONS
(¹/₂" seams allowed)

1 *Cutting:* From voile, cut an 11" square
pillow front and two 6" x 11" pillow backs.

2 *Pillow Front:* Pin four 11" lengths of
insertion lace to the voile pillow front,
symmetrically spaced as shown;
edgestitch. With small, sharp scissors, cut
away the voile behind the lace. Place the
right side of the satin square against the
wrong side of the pillow front, with edges
even. Baste the edges.

3 *Piping:* Pin the piping ¹/₂" from the
edges of the pillow front, with right sides
together and raw edges outward, clipping
to the piping seam at each corner. Stitch
over the piping seam.

4 *Ruffle:* Seam the short ends of the
ruffle lace together; press seam open.
Fold the resulting loop with the seam at
one end and mark the opposite fold. Fold
the loop in half again and mark those two
folds. Stitch a gathering row at each quarter
(mark to mark) of the loop. Pin the lace to
the pillow front with the seam or a quarter
mark at each corner; have right sides
together and raw edges even. Pull up
gathers to fit the pillow. Stitch along the
piping seam.

5 *Pillow Back:* With right sides facing,
pin the two back pieces together along an
11" edge. Stitch a ¹/₂"-long seam at each
end. Press the seams and apply a zipper
between them. Open the zipper partway.

6 *Assembly:* Pushing lace toward the
center, pin pillow front to pillow back, with
right sides together and edges even. Seam
along the previous stitching. Turn the case
right side out through the zipper opening.

7 *Ring Ribbons:* Cut two 8" lengths of
ribbon. Pin the center of each to the pillow
as shown and fasten them in place with
small stitches.

8 Insert the pillow form and close the
zipper. Tie a ribbon around each ring.

CAMISOLE
AND TAP PANTS

Every bride will feel very special on her wedding day in this satin and lace camisole set.

Average: For those with some experience in sewing.

Luscious lingerie, in lace-trimmed satin is the perfect choice for the bride's trousseau. We've chosen soft, apple-blossom pink but you might prefer pure white.

MATERIALS
- ☐ 2¹/₄ **yds. of 45"-wide silk satin**
- ☐ **6 yds. of double-edged lace**
- ☐ **elastic for panties**
- ☐ **1 yd. round silk cord for shoulder straps**
- ☐ **Optional: embroidery floss, in shades of pink and green**

DIRECTIONS

1 *To Enlarge a Pattern:* Draw a series of vertical lines 2" apart. At right angles to these, draw a series of horizontal lines 2" apart to complete the grid of 2" squares. Now copy the four pattern pieces on page 36 to your own grid, imitating the lines one square at a time. Copy all the grain lines and labels.

2 *Cutting:* Pin the patterns to the wrong side of the satin, leaving an empty inch between pieces (for seam allowances, which are not included in the pattern). *You will cut ¹/₂" outside the pattern lines.* Place the pattern pieces so the grainlines are parallel to the lengthwise (selvedge) threads. Where "a pair" is called for, pin the pattern once with its right side up and once with its wrong side up. Notice that the two camisole pieces are cut with the center edge on a fold of fabric. Cut out the six pieces as instructed.

3 *Seaming:* Stitch ¹/₂" seams with right sides together and zigzag stitch the raw edges to prevent fraying. OR, make French seams this way: stitch ¹/₄" seams with the wrong sides together, then turn the piece wrong side out and stitch again to enclose the raw edges.

4 *Camisole:* Seam the camisole front to camisole back at the side edges, ending just before the curve begins.

5 *Lace:* Pin lace over the right side of the camisole at top and bottom. With a machine straight stitch, edgestitch the inner edges of each piece of lace. Cover this straight stitching with a deep machine zigzag stitch. If your don't have a zigzag stitch, make another row of straight stitching ¹/₈" outside the first one. With sharp embroidery scissors, cut away the satin that shows behind the lace, leaving a ¹/₄" satin seam allowance.

6 *Straps:* Cut two 18" straps from the round cord. Pin one end of each under the top back edge of the camisole, equidistant from the center back. Try on the camisole and pin the front ends in place. Remove the camisole and sew the four ends securely in place.

7 *Tap Pants:* Seam each Tap Pant Front to a Tap Pant Back at the long outside seam. Seam the resulting two pieces together at the CF and CB seams. Stitch a casing at the top edge and insert elastic to fit your waist. Sew lace to the lower edge (see Step 5, above). Stitch the inside leg seams.

8 *Optional Embroidery:* Embroider roses, as shown, if you wish (see page 37).

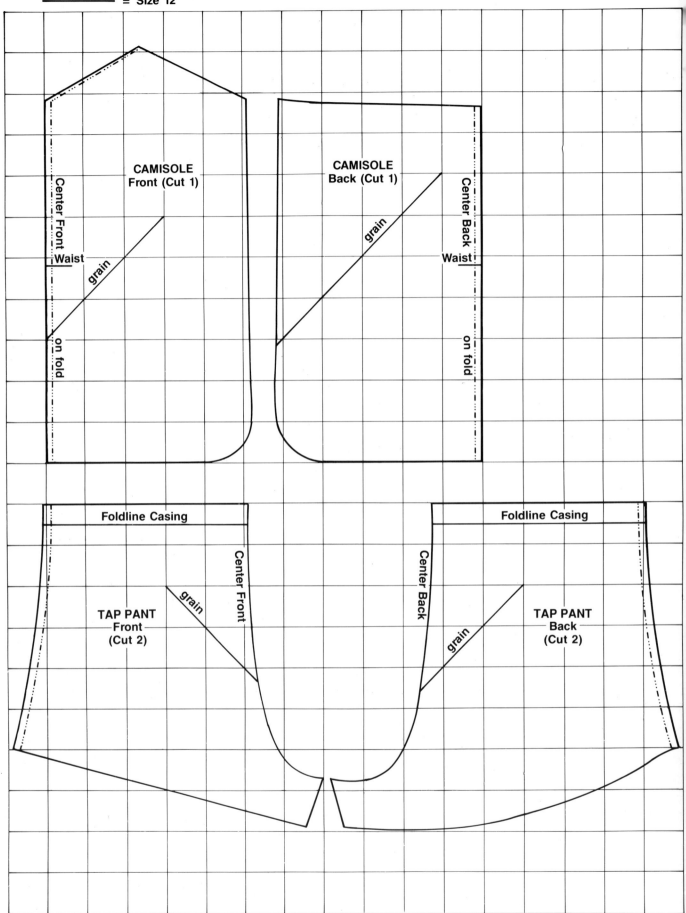

Size 10
Size 12

CAMISOLE
Front (Cut 1)

Center Front

Waist

grain

on fold

CAMISOLE
Back (Cut 1)

grain

Center Back

Waist

on fold

Foldline Casing

TAP PANT
Front
(Cut 2)

grain

Center Front

Center Back

grain

Foldline Casing

TAP PANT
Back
(Cut 2)

Each square is 2 inches.

❖ HOW TO EMBROIDER ROSE BUDS ❖

These rosebuds are stitched in graduated tones of stranded cotton, starting at the center with the darkest shade and working outward to the lightest shade. You can stitch leaves in bullion knots as well, or make a green chain stitch. The stems are shown in outline stitch. They could be small chain or back stitches (see page 23).

Bring needle up at A. Take a stitch from B to A (Fig. 1); do not pull the needle through (A to B equals the length of knot). Twist thread several times around the needle, to equal the A to B width (Fig. 2). Pull the needle through, easing the twists of thread against each other over the core thread. Re-insert the needle at B (Fig. 3) to start the next stitch. Cluster the bullion knots as shown below (Fig. 4).

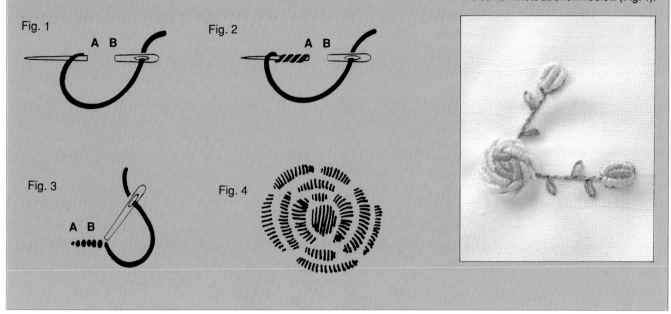

Fig. 1

A B

Fig. 2

A B

Fig. 3

A B

Fig. 4

Right: It is quite easy to achieve the border on the camisole and tap pants. Once the inside edge of the lace has been stitched to the satin garment, the fabric behind the lace can be cut away close to the stitchline. Use a sharp pair of small scissors and be careful not to cut through the lace or the stitches.

SWEET NOTHINGS

Make something delicate and beautiful especially for the bride. These lovely boudoir items are just the thing. Fragrant shoe stuffers, matching padded hanger and jewelry bundle are all made in a very Victorian print. Team them with the luxurious quilted lingerie bag and lavender sachet and she'll treasure them forever.

❖ QUILTED LINGERIE CASE ❖

Average: For those with some experience in sewing.

MATERIALS
- ☐ **18" x 28" each of quilted silk and of lining fabric**
- ☐ **1³/₄ yds. of satin piping**
- ☐ **³/₄ yd. or ribbon**

DIRECTIONS

1   *Marking:* On the quilted piece, draw the same curve at both ends of an 18" edge. Cut the curved corners, then the lining to match. From the opposite, straight end measure upward 9" and mark this at each long side edge.

2   *Piping:* Pin the piping to the quilted piece, with right sides together and raw edges even. Start at one 9" mark and pin up to and across the top and down to the opposite 9" mark, turning both raw ends down into the seam to hide the raw edges. Stitch on the piping seam.

3   *Lining:* Pin the quilted piece to the lining, right sides together and edges even. Stitch over the piping seam. Continue to stitch the unpiped edges, leaving an open-ing at the bottom edge for turning. Turn the piece right side out. Turn in and slipstitch the open edges and press.

4   *Case:* Fold the lower edge upward, right side out, at the ends of the piping. By hand, securely slipstitch the bag's side edges against the piping to make the pocket of the case.

5   *Ribbon:* Cut the ribbon in half. Turn in one raw end and sew it securely to the underside of the flap center. Fold the flap down and mark a position for the opposite ribbon. Turn in and sew one end of that ribbon to the case. Tie a bow.

❖ MONOGRAMMED ❖ LAVENDER SACHET

Average: For those with some experience in sewing.

MATERIALS
- ☐ **¹/₄ yd. 36"-wide silk taffeta**
- ☐ **1 yd. of cord or narrow ribbon**
- ☐ **dried lavender leaves**
- ☐ **embroidery floss**
- **Optional: permanent-color fabric marker, tailor's chalk, or dressmaker's carbon and dry ballpoint pen**

DIRECTIONS

1   *Cutting:* From taffeta, cut two 5" x 9¹/₂" rectangles for bag front and back and a 2" x 35" ruffle strip. Place the rectangles together with edges even. Fold them in half lengthwise and cut a curve at one corner (see photo).

2   *Monogram:* Transfer a monogram to the bag front (see Step 6 on page 22 and the alphabet on page 25). We first traced the initials, through dressmaker's carbon paper, to the taffeta. Within the outlines we colored the letters with a fabric marker. When that had dried, we covered the outline with a row of small chain stitches. Instead, you could fill in the whole letter with continuous chain stitches.

3   *Pleated Ruffle:* Fold the ruffle strip in half lengthwise with the wrong sides together. Pleat the raw edges. Starting 2⁵/₈" from the top edge, pin the ruffle around the side and bottom edges of the bag front with right sides together and raw edges even. Turn each ruffle end down into the seam so the raw edges disappear. Stitch the ruffle.

Quilted Lingerie Bag, Monogrammed Lavender Sachet

4 *Bag:* Pin bag back to bag front, over the ruffle, with right sides together and raw edges even. Stitch through the previous stitching. Turn the bag right side out and press. At the top edge turn in 2⅝" and slipstitch a hem. Fill the bag with lavender. Tie a cord or ribbon around the bag to close it.

❖ FLORAL COVERED HANGER ❖

Average: For those with some experience in sewing.

MATERIALS
- [ ] **standard wooden coat hanger**
- [ ] **four 3½" x 40" strips of printed voile**
- [ ] **synthetic batting**

DIRECTIONS
1 *Batting:* Wrap batting around the wooden hanger and sew it smoothly in place by hand. It should measure about 4" around in girth.
2 *Seaming:* The voile will be used double. So stack two layers right side up, then two more layers right side up. Pin one stack over the other with right sides together and edges even. Mark, 1" each side of top center, an opening for the hanger hook. Seam (³/₈") the rest of the edges together. Turn the layers right side out through the opening; press.
3 *Gathering:* Topstitch a row of gathering stitches ¼" from the seams. Slide the hanger into the cover, one end at a time. Draw up the gathering to fit the hanger and tie the thread ends. By hand, sew a short gathering row across the open edges, pull it up to fit and fasten the ends.
4 *Hook:* Fold a 1½" x 14" strip of voile in half lengthwise with right sides together. Stich ¼" from the long raw edge and around one short end. Trim the seam allowance to ⅛" wide. Turn the strip right side out and press it, with the seam at one edge. Sew a gathering row ⅛" from each long edge. Draw the cover over the hook, pull up the gathers to fit and sew its lower end to the hanger cover. Tie a bow around its base, it you like.

❖ SCENTED SHOE STUFFER ❖

Easy: Achievable by anyone.

MATERIALS (for each stuffer)
- [ ] **two 5" x 9½" fabric rectangles**
- [ ] **2"-wide fabric strip 1 yd. long for**

Floral Hanger, Scented Shoe Stuffers

- [ ] **ruffle**
- [ ] **lavender or potpourri**

DIRECTIONS
1 *Toe:* Place the fabric rectangles together with edges even. Fold them in half lengthwise and cut one corner to form half of the toe-shape (see photo).
2 *Ruffle:* Fold the ruffle strip in half lengthwise, wrong sides together and press. Sew a gathering row along the raw edges. Measuring from the top (straight) edge of a fabric rectangle, mark 3" down each side edge. Starting at this mark, pin the ruffle to one piece of fabric with right sides together and raw edges even. Turn each end into the seam to conceal the raw edges. Pull up the gathers to fit the stuffer edges, adjust the fulness evenly and stitch on the gathering line.
3 *Stuffer:* Pin the fabric rectangles right sides together, over ruffle, and stitch through the previous stitching. Turn the stuffer right side out and stitch a ¼" hem at the top edge.
4 *Finishing:* Fill the stuffer with lavender. Tie a cord or ribbon around it at the top of the ruffle.

❖ SLEEP PILLOW ❖

Average: For those with some experience in sewing.

Fill this pretty pillow with wonderful scents and relaxing herbs to hang from your bed or slip under your pillow.

MATERIALS
- ☐ 1/2 yd. 44"-wide fabric
- ☐ a 9 1/2" square of organza (or similar)
- ☐ 3/4 yd. of cord or ribbon for bow and hanger
- ☐ dried herbs and flowers

DIRECTIONS
1 *Cutting:* From the fabric, cut one 9 1/2" square, one 5" square and two 2 1/4"-wide ruffle strips — one 36" long and one 64" long. Fold each square in half, right sides together and pin the edges. Draw half a heart with its center on the fold, then cut along the drawn line through both layers. Cut the organza to match the larger fabric heart.

2 *Ruffle:* Seam the short ends of each ruffle to make a loop. Fold the loop in half lengthwise wrong sides together, and pleat the raw edges together by hand or machine. With right sides together and edges even, sew the longer ruffle to the large heart and the shorter ruffle to the small heart.

3 *Organza:* On the small heart, turn under the raw edges and press them toward the center. Then sew the heart, through the ruffle seam, to the center of the organza heart.

4 *Assembly:* Pin the large floral heart to the organza (over the ruffles and the small heart) right side together. Stitch around the edges, leaving an opening (on one of the straighter edges) for turning. Turn the heart right side out, clipping the curved seam, and press.

5 *Finishing:* Into the opening, push flowers or herbs under the organza. From cord or ribbon, make a loop about 5" long. Insert both ends into the opening and sew them securely. Close the opening by hand. Tie a bow and sew it to the smaller heart.

❖ JEWELRY POUCH ❖

Average: For those with some experience in sewing.

MATERIALS
- ☐ 1 yd. 44"-wide fabric
- ☐ 1 3/4 yd. cord or ribbon

DIRECTIONS (3/8" seams allowed)
1 *Cutting:* From the fabric, cut two 18"-dia. and two 13"-dia. circles, one 2" x 44" ruffle strip and another 2" x 34".

2 *Ruffle:* Fold each ruffle strip in half lengthwise, wrong sides together and press. Gather the raw edges. With right sides together and raw edges even, pin the longer strip to a large circle and the shorter strip to a small circle, distributing the fulness evenly, and stitch along the gathering row.

3 *Pouch:* With right sides together and edges even, seam the matching circles together with the ruffle between, leaving an opening for turning. Turn right side out and press.

4 *Pockets:* Pin the small circle over the larger one, with centers matching. Draw a vertical and a horizontal diameter across the small circle. Then draw two more halfway between the first ones; stitch across the lines to make eight pockets. Fasten the thread ends securely at the ends of each stitchline.

5. *Casing:* Draw two lines, one 1 1/2" and the other 2" from the outer edge of the larger circle. Topstitch along the two drawn circles to make the casing. Within the casing, by hand make two vertical buttonholes about 1/2" apart, *through the outside fabric only.* Push the cord through the casing. Tie a knot at each end of the cord. Draw up the circle into a pouch.

Sleep Pillow, Floral Jewelry Pouch

❖ LACE-COVERED BOX ❖

Average: For those with some experience in crafting.

MATERIALS
- ☐ **oval balsa wood or cardboard box, about 7" x 10" x 4" high**
- ☐ **fabric remnants to underline the lace (we used pink silk taffeta)**
- ☐ **about 1³/₄ yds. of lace at least 8" wide, finished at both edges**
- ☐ **synthetic batting**
- ☐ **about 2 yds. ¹/₁₆" ribbon**
- ☐ **white glue**
- ☐ **Optional: 3 satin ribbon roses for lid center**

DIRECTIONS

1 *Cutting:* To the wrong side of the fabric, trace the box lid three times, leaving 1¹/₂" of space between tracings; cut out three ovals ³/₄" ouside the traced lines. Cut a "box sides" piece in the following length and depth: For length, measure around the box and add 2"; for depth, measure from the outside bottom, up to the top, then down again to the inside bottom and add 2". Cut a "lid sides" piece, measuring the lid as you did the box and adding 2" to each dimension.

2 *Batting:* Cover the box with the lid, then trace the edge of the lid to the box. Glue batting to the box from the drawn line downward and for about an inch over the bottom edge, clipping out the extra fulness. Glue an oval of batting over the bottom. Glue batting to the outer side of the lid and 1" over the top, clipping the edge. Glue an oval of batting to the lip top.

3 *Box Bottom:* Glue one fabric oval to the inside box bottom, turning the edges up to the sides, clipping the curves so the fabric will lie flat. Glue another fabric oval to the outside bottom in the same way then sew the fabric edges to the batting by hand.

4 *Box Sides:* At one long edge of the wide fabric strip, turn under ¹/₂" and press; do the same at one short edge. Place the long turned-under edge along the box bottom; wrap the piece around the box, overlapping the raw end with the turned under end. Slipstitch the turned-under edges. At the top of the box, turn the fabric down inside to the bottom and mark a cutting line around the base. Cut on the cutting line and glue down cut edge.

5 *Box Lid:* Cover the box lid and the box lid sides with fabric the same way you covered the box in Steps 3 and 4.

6 *Lace:* Cut two strips of the lace, each 2" longer than the box circumference. Wrap one piece up and over the box sides with one scalloped edge near the outside bottom and the other near the inside bottom. Turn under the final raw ends and lap it over the first end, slipstitching it in place. Glue the lace edges in place. Wrap the other length of lace around the lid with one finished edge at the edge of the lip. Turn under the final end and lap it over the first end. Slipstitch it in place and continue to sew the seam through the extending lace. Glue the lace to the lip. Gather up the opposite edge in the center of the lid, wrapping the gathers with thread and sewing through them several times. Let the loose edge make a central ruffle in the middle of which you can sew ribbon roses (see page 61) if you like.

7 *Ribbon:* Glue the narrow ribbon around the lid and the box (see photo), turning under the overlapping end.

❖ BONBONS

Beautiful bonbons, filled with potpourri or lavender are so easy to make. Why not make a simple lavender bag from the same lace for a pretty set.

Easy: Achievable by anyone.

MATERIALS (for each)
- ☐ **6" length of 8"-wide double-edged lace**
- ☐ **6" x 8" tulle for lining**
- ☐ **¹/₂ yd. decorative ribbon, for trimming**
- ☐ **potpourri or lavender**

DIRECTIONS

1 *Seaming:* Place tulle against the wrong side of the lace with edges even. With the tulle side out, fold them (as one fabric) to bring the raw edges together. Seam the raw edges and press the seam open with your thumb nail. Turn the tube right side out.

2 *Filling:* With half the ribbon, tie a bow around the tube at one end. Fill the bonbon with potpourri, then tie a bow to close the other end.

THE WEDDING CAKE

A slice of happiness is guaranteed for each and every guest with these three wedding cakes. It's the decoration that whets the appetite and recreates the memory.

❖ TIERED CAKE ❖

Makes one ¹/₂ pound layer.
CAKE
- [ ] **3 cups golden raisins**
- [ ] **1¹/₂ cups raisins**
- [ ] **1²/₃ cups currants**
- [ ] **³/₄ cup glacé cherries, chopped**
- [ ] **³/₄ cup glacé mixed fruit**
- [ ] **³/₄ cup brandy**
- [ ] **1 teaspoon grated lemon rind**
- [ ] **1 cup (2 sticks) butter or margarine, softened**
- [ ] **1¹/₂ cups firmly packed brown sugar**
- [ ] **4 eggs**
- [ ] **1 tablespoon honey**

- [ ] **1 tablespoon orange marmalade**
- [ ] **3 cups unsifted all-purpose flour**
- [ ] **1 teaspoon ground allspice**
- [ ] **1 teaspoon ground cinnamon**
- [ ] **¹/₄ cup apple jelly, melted**
MARZIPAN
- [ ] **1¹/₄ cup blanched whole almonds**
- [ ] **3 cups IOX (confectioners') sugar, sifted**
- [ ] **¹/₃ cup light corn syrup**
- [ ] **2 tablespoons lemon juice**
- [ ] **1 tablespoon glycerine**
- [ ] **1 tablespoon sweet sherry**
- [ ] **1 to 2 drops almond extract (optional)**
COVERING FONDANT
- [ ] **1 tablespoon unflavored gelatin**

- [ ] **3 tablespoons cold water**
- [ ] **¹/₂ cup liquid glucose**
- [ ] **1 tablespoon glycerine**
- [ ] **6 IOX (confectioners') sugar, sifted**
- [ ] **Decorating Frosting (recipe follows)**
- [ ] **food coloring (optional)**

1   Preheat the oven to slow (300°). Lightly grease and flour one 8 or 9 x 3-inch round, one 8 x 2-inch square or one 9 x 2-inch petal shaped cake pan.

2   To prepare the cake, combine the raisins, currants, cherries, mixed fruit, brandy and lemon rind in a large bowl. Mix well, cover and refrigerate, stirring occasionally

for 2 to 3 days.

3 Cream butter and sugar in a large bowl until light and fluffy. Add eggs one at a time, beating well after each addition. Beat in marmalade and honey.

4 Sift together the flour, allspice and cinnamon on a sheet of waxed paper. Alternately add to the creamed mixture with the marinated fruit, stirring until well blended.

5 Spoon mixture into the prepared pan. Bake in the preheated slow oven (300°) for 3½ to 4 hours, or until a cake tester inserted in the center comes out clean.

6 Remove the cake from the oven and cool upright in pan on a wire rack for 30 minutes. Invert on rack, turn right side up and cool thoroughly. Wet a piece of cheesecloth, large enough to encase the cake with the remaining brandy and completely wrap the cake. To bake additional layers, follow the chart (page 45).

7 To prepare the Marzipan: Place the almonds in the container of an electric food processor or blender. Whirl at high speed until a smooth paste is obtained. Add the IOX (confectioners') sugar and whirl until the mixture is combined. Add the lemon juice, glycerine, sherry and almond extract and whirl about 30 seconds, or until well blended. The mixture should hold together when pressed between your fingers. If mixture seems too dry, add light corn syrup, ¼ teaspoon at a time, continuing to whirl until a smooth dough-like consistency is obtained. If mixture seems too soft, whirl in additional IOX (confectioners') sugar, 1 tablespoon at a time.

8 To prepare the Covering Fondant: Sprinkle gelatin over water in a 1-cup heat proof glass measure and let sit for 5 minutes. Place gelatin mixture in a small saucepan of water. Bring to a simmer over low heat, stirring until the gelatin is dissolved. Add the glucose and glycerine and stir until well blended. Remove the gelatin mixture from the water and cool slightly.

9 Place the IOX (confectioners') sugar in a large mixing bowl. Make a well in the center and pour in the gelatin mixture. Using a lightly greased wooden spoon, stir in the mixture until blended. With lightly greased hands, knead mixture in the bowl until most of the sugar is incorporated. Turn out onto a smooth, lightly greased surface such as a marble slab or plastic laminated counter and knead until smooth, pliable and satiny.

10 For ease in rolling, wrap the fondant tightly in an airtight plastic bag and leave at room temperature for at least 24 hours.

11 To assemble the Cake: Invert the bottom layer onto a carboard the same diameter as the layer. Divide the Marzipan in half. Roll out one half between 2 sheets of

❖ PREPARING THE CAKE ❖

1 To achieve good evenly shaped cakes, line cake pans with heavy duty aluminium foil, placing shiny side against pan and dull side against cake. Cut three strips of newspaper 1 inch wider than sides of cake pan. Position strips around cake pan and secure with string. This acts as an insulator preventing outside edge of cakes from burning.

2 Turn out cake onto covered board. Fill any fruit holes or creases in cake with small pieces of marzipan and smooth out with a spatula. Roll out remaining marzipan and place over cake smoothing sides. Trim away excess.

3 Roll out fondant to fit cake size and lift onto cake. Smooth out and trim excess fondant from cake base using photo as a guide.

4 To assemble cakes, mark positions for pillars on top of larger cake. Insert thick wooden skewers right through cake to board. Place pillars over skewers and position top cake tier.

plastic wrap into a thin circle the size of the diameter of the bottom layer, plus the depth of the layer plus 3 inches. Example: if the cake is 9 x 2-inches, roll the Marzipan to a 14-inch round. Use a 14-inch round pan or a round cut from a piece of cardboard for a guide. Remove the plastic wrap. Use a sharp knife or pizza cutter and cut an even round circle. If using a 14-inch round cake pan, lightly grease before setting on the Marzipan.

12 For ease in applying the Marzipan to the cake, transfer the Marzipan to a large cookie sheet. Recover the top with plastic wrap and freeze it for a few minutes to make it less flexible.

13 Brush the bottom cake layer with a thin coating of the melted apple jelly.

14 Supporting the Marzipan with your hands, position it over the bottom layer and lay it on the top and sides of the cake. Do not move once it has been placed, however, it may be smoothed out with your hands. Trim away any excess Marzipan.

15 To apply the Covering Fondant, roll enough fondant for the bottom layer on a lightly greased surface to a circle the same size as the Marzipan circle, rotating every 2 to 3 rolls to prevent sticking and being careful not to pull the fondant as it will tear. To keep from drying out, cover the fondant

with plastic wrap.

16 Lightly brush the Marzipan surface with a thin coating of melted apple jelly.

17 Carefully lift the fondant over the cake. Quickly smooth out any wrinkles with the palm of your hand, working from the center in a circular motion to prevent air bubbles.

18 Using a small sharp knife, or pizza cutter, trim the fondant at the base even with the Marzipan.

19 Divide frosting into small bowls. Tint with desired food coloring. Keep bowls covered with damp paper toweling to prevent drying out.

20 Spoon frosting into pastry bags fitted with decorative tips and decorate as desired.

21 To assemble cakes, mark positions for pillars on top of larger cake. Insert thick wooden skewers right through cake to board. Place pillars over skewers and position on top cake tier.

Decorating Frosting: Prepare one recipe Royal Icing according to directions on label of container of meringue powder.

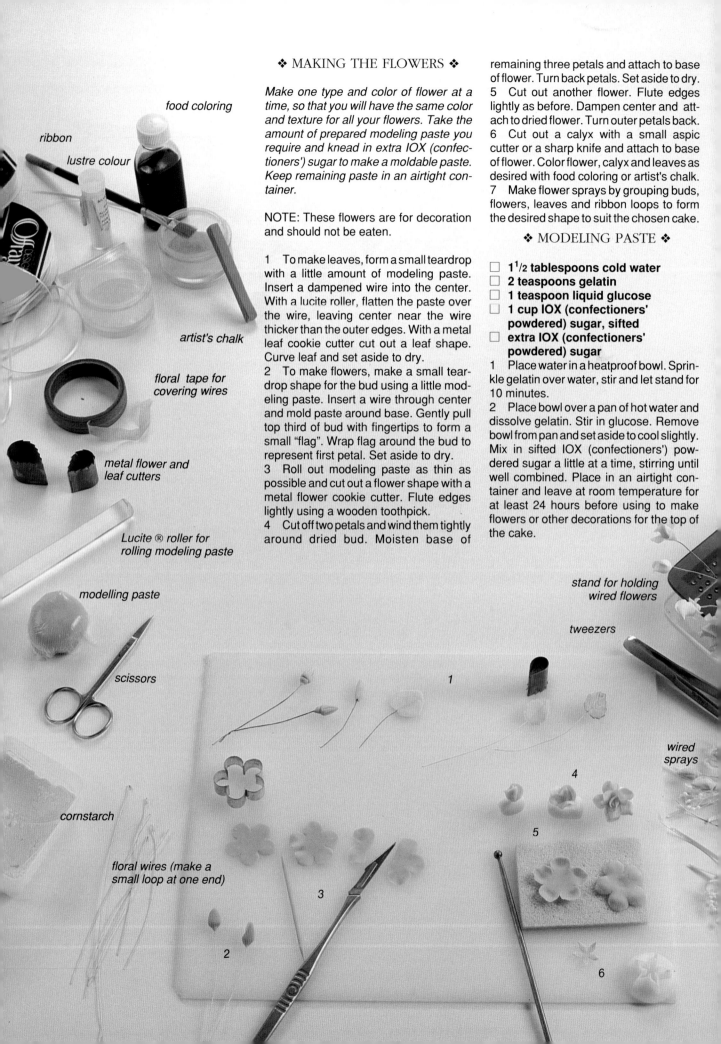

food coloring

ribbon

lustre colour

artist's chalk

floral tape for covering wires

metal flower and leaf cutters

Lucite ® roller for rolling modeling paste

modelling paste

scissors

cornstarch

floral wires (make a small loop at one end)

stand for holding wired flowers

tweezers

wired sprays

❖ MAKING THE FLOWERS ❖

Make one type and color of flower at a time, so that you will have the same color and texture for all your flowers. Take the amount of prepared modeling paste you require and knead in extra IOX (confectioners') sugar to make a moldable paste. Keep remaining paste in an airtight container.

NOTE: These flowers are for decoration and should not be eaten.

1   To make leaves, form a small teardrop with a little amount of modeling paste. Insert a dampened wire into the center. With a lucite roller, flatten the paste over the wire, leaving center near the wire thicker than the outer edges. With a metal leaf cookie cutter cut out a leaf shape. Curve leaf and set aside to dry.
2   To make flowers, make a small teardrop shape for the bud using a little modeling paste. Insert a wire through center and mold paste around base. Gently pull top third of bud with fingertips to form a small "flag". Wrap flag around the bud to represent first petal. Set aside to dry.
3   Roll out modeling paste as thin as possible and cut out a flower shape with a metal flower cookie cutter. Flute edges lightly using a wooden toothpick.
4   Cut off two petals and wind them tightly around dried bud. Moisten base of remaining three petals and attach to base of flower. Turn back petals. Set aside to dry.
5   Cut out another flower. Flute edges lightly as before. Dampen center and attach to dried flower. Turn outer petals back.
6   Cut out a calyx with a small aspic cutter or a sharp knife and attach to base of flower. Color flower, calyx and leaves as desired with food coloring or artist's chalk.
7   Make flower sprays by grouping buds, flowers, leaves and ribbon loops to form the desired shape to suit the chosen cake.

❖ MODELING PASTE ❖

☐ **1¹/₂ tablespoons cold water**
☐ **2 teaspoons gelatin**
☐ **1 teaspoon liquid glucose**
☐ **1 cup IOX (confectioners' powdered) sugar, sifted**
☐ **extra IOX (confectioners' powdered) sugar**

1   Place water in a heatproof bowl. Sprinkle gelatin over water, stir and let stand for 10 minutes.
2   Place bowl over a pan of hot water and dissolve gelatin. Stir in glucose. Remove bowl from pan and set aside to cool slightly. Mix in sifted IOX (confectioners') powdered sugar a little at a time, stirring until well combined. Place in an airtight container and leave at room temperature for at least 24 hours before using to make flowers or other decorations for the top of the cake.

WEDDING CAKE CHART

CAKE SIZE	125 g ($^1/_4$ lb)	250 g ($^1/_2$ lb)	375 g ($^3/_4$ lb)	500 g (1 lb)	625 g (1 $^1/_4$ lb)	750 g (1$^1/_2$ lb)
golden raisins	1$^1/_2$ cups	3 cups	4$^1/_2$ cups	6 cups	7$^1/_2$ cups	9 cups
raisins	$^3/_4$ cup	1$^1/_2$ cups	2$^1/_4$ cups	3 cups	3$^3/_4$ cups	4$^1/_2$ cups
currants	$^3/_4$ cup	1$^1/_2$ cups	2$^1/_4$ cups	3 cups	3$^3/_4$ cups	4$^1/_2$ cups
mixed peel	$^1/_4$ cup	$^3/_4$ cup	1 cup	1$^1/_2$ cups	1$^3/_4$ cups	2$^1/_4$ cups
glacé (candied) cherries	$^1/_4$ cup	$^3/_4$ cup	1 cup	1$^1/_2$ cups	1$^3/_4$ cups	2$^1/_4$ cups
grated lemon zest	1 tsp	1 tsp	1 tsp	2 tsps	1 tbsp	1 tbsp
brandy, sherry	$^1/_4$ cup	$^1/_3$ cup	$^3/_4$ cup	1 cup	1$^1/_3$ cups	1$^2/_3$ cup
butter	$^1/_2$ cup (1 stick) plus 2 tablespoons	1 cup (2 sticks) plus 2 tablespoons	1$^1/_2$ cups (3 sticks) plus 2 tablespoons	2 cups (4 sticks)	2$^1/_2$ cups (5 sticks)	3 cups (6 sticks)
firmly packed light brown sugar	$^2/_3$ cup	1$^1/_3$ cups	1$^3/_4$ cups	2$^2/_3$ cups	3 cups	4 cups
eggs	2	4	6	8	10	12
marmalade	2 tsps	1 tbsp	1$^1/_2$ tbsps	2 tbsps	2 $^1/_2$ tbsps	3 tbsps
honey	2 tsps	1 tbsp	1$^1/_2$ tbsps	2 tbsps	2 $^1/_2$ tbsps	3 tbsps
glycerine	1 tsp	2 tsps	1 tbsp	1 tbsp	1$^1/_4$ tbsps	1$^1/_2$ tbsps
all-purpose flour	1$^1/_2$ cups	3 cups	4$^1/_2$ cups	6 cups	7$^1/_2$ cups	9 cups
ground all-spice	$^1/_2$ tsp	1 tsp	1 $^1/_2$ tsps	2 tsps	2$^1/_2$ tsps	1 tbsp
cinnamon	$^1/_2$ tsp	1 tsp	1 $^1/_2$ tsps	2 tsps	2$^1/_2$ tsps	1 tbsp
PAN SIZE						
deep round (diameter)	6-7"	9"	11"	12"	13"	14"
deep square	6-7"	8"	9"	10"	12"	14"
BAKING TIMES at 300°F (in hours)						
	3-3$^1/_2$	3$^1/_2$-4	4- 4$^1/_2$	4 $^1/_2$-5	5$^1/_2$-6	7-7$^1/_2$

MERINGUE FROSTING
- [ ] **1¼ cups sugar**
- [ ] **½ cup water**
- [ ] **3 egg whites**
- [ ] **½ teaspoon almond extract**
- [ ] **food coloring (optional)**

1   To prepare the cake, combine the golden raisins, currants, raisins, peel, glacé cherries and mixed fruit, carrot, butter, brown sugar, brandy and orange juice in a large saucepan. Cook over medium heat, without boiling, stirring constantly until sugar is dissolved.

2   Bring mixture to a boil, reduce heat to low and simmer for 10 minutes. Transfer mixture to a large bowl and allow to cool to room temperature.

3   Meanwhile, preheat the oven to slow (300°). Generously grease and flour a simulated bell shaped 9-cup steam pudding mold.

4   On a sheet of waxed paper, combine flour, self-rising flour and baking soda; reserve.

5   Stir in eggs, corn syrup and orange rind into the cooled fruit mixture. Fold in the dry ingredients.

6   Divide the batter equally between the two prepared pans. Place on a large baking sheet, or a 15½ x 10½ x 1-inch baking pan.

7   Bake in the preheated slow oven (300°) for 1 hour, or until a cake tester inserted in the center comes out clean.

8   Cool in the pan on a wire rack for 15 minutes. Carefully loosen around the sides, using a thin metal spatula; invert onto the rack. Cool completely. Wrap tightly with aluminum foil until ready to frost.

9   To prepare the Meringue Frosting, combine the sugar and water in a large saucepan. Cook over medium heat, without boiling, stirring constantly until the sugar dissolves. Brush any sugar from sides of pan using a pastry brush dipped in water.

10 Bring syrup to the boil and boil rapidly for 3 to 5 minutes, without stirring or until syrup reaches the soft ball stage or 230° on a candy thermometer.

11 Beat the egg whites until stiff peaks form. Continue beating while pouring in syrup in a thin stream a little at a time. Continue beating until all the syrup is used and the frosting will stand in stiff peaks.

12 Add almond extract and desired amount of food coloring if using. Beat to blend well.

13 Frost the sides and top of the cake with frosting, shaping the frosting to resemble a bell.

14 Decorate the top of the cake with fresh, dried or silk flowers. Make frame as instructed in the Heart Shaped Frame (on page 47), decorate and position over the cake.

❖ WEDDING BELL CAKE ❖

To obtain a simulated bell-shaped cake, we used a 9-cup steam pudding mold to bake the cake in. A small 5 to 6 cup stainless steel dome shaped mixing bowl may also be used.

Makes 25 servings or two 1 pound cakes.

CAKE
- [ ] **3 cups golden raisins**
- [ ] **2 cups currants**
- [ ] **2 cups raisins**
- [ ] **1 cup dried mixed citrus peel**
- [ ] **1 cup glacé cherries, halved**
- [ ] **½ cup chopped glacé mixed fruit**
- [ ] **1 carrot, grated**
- [ ] **1½ cups (3 sticks) butter or margarine, softened**
- [ ] **1½ cups firmly packed light brown sugar**
- [ ] **¾ cup brandy**
- [ ] **¾ cup orange juice**
- [ ] **2½ cups sifted all-purpose flour**
- [ ] **½ cup sifted self-rising flour**
- [ ] **1 teaspoon baking soda**
- [ ] **7 eggs, slightly beaten**
- [ ] **1½ tablespoons honey**
- [ ] **1 tablespoon grated orange rind**

❖ HEART SHAPED FRAME ❖

MATERIALS

- [ ] **2 squares of $^1/_2$-inch-thick wood or particle board approximately twice the height of the cake.**
- [ ] jigsaw or scroll saw
- [ ] baby's breath
- [ ] fresh or dried flowers
- [ ] several yards of 1-inch wide and $^1/_4$-inch-wide satin ribbon
- [ ] wood glue
- [ ] floral wire
- [ ] cardboard and pencil for patterns

DIRECTIONS

1   On cardboard, using photo as a guide, draw a heart pattern 2 or 3 inches taller than twice the height of the cake, and then a concentric heart about 1 inch inside the first. Using the photo on page 46 as a guide, square off the upper point of the heart so the squared-off edge is about 1 inch wide. Cut out the pattern and then cut straight across the pattern, about 3 inches above the bottom point, so that the base of the heart will fit comfortably around the base of the cake.

2   Use the pattern to cut out two heart frames from wood. Be sure the bases of the frames are perfectly flat. From one frame, cut out a $^1/_2$-inch-wide notch in one point, using photo as a guide. The point of one heart will fit into the notch of the other, at right angles.

3   Wrap 1-inch-wide ribbon around the entire frame to cover it. Secure with glue. Place one frame in notch of the other at right angles and secure with glue.

4   Tie $^1/_4$-inch-wide ribbon bows evenly spaced around the entire frame. Tuck baby's breath or flowers into the ribbon bows. Secure with glue.

5   Wire small bunches of fresh or dried flowers together, and then wire them to the center of the heart, covering the join. Add ribbon bows.

6   Position the frame around the cake. Use frosting or modeling paste (page 44) to hold it in place and cover base with more flowers.

❖ HEART-TO-HEART ❖ WEDDING CAKE

You will need to make this recipe two times for the three heart shaped cakes. One portion will fit into the largest pan and the other is divided proportionately between the two other pans. To get the high cakes shown in the photograph (page 48) prepare and bake the cake two or three separate times depending on the height desired. Place desired number of layers together to obtain desired height. Fill and frost. It may be necessary to make up extra batches of frosting.

We have used deep heart-shaped cake pans measuring 8-inches, 9-inches and 12-inches, which are available from speciality cake decorating suppliers. If not available, comparable-sized round cake pans may be substituted.

CAKE
- ☐ **1 cup (2 sticks plus 2 tbsps) butter or margarine, softened**
- ☐ **2¼ cups sugar**
- ☐ **2 teaspoons vanilla extract**
- ☐ **6 eggs**
- ☐ **2 cups sifted all-purpose flour**
- ☐ **¾ cup sifted self-rising flour**
- ☐ **¾ cup milk**
- ☐ **3 egg whites**

BUTERCREAM FROSTING
- ☐ **1 cup (2 sticks plus 2 tbsps) butter or margarine, softened**
- ☐ **½ cup milk**
- **2 teaspoons almond extract**
- **2 teaspoons vanilla extract**
- ☐ **10½ cups unsifted IOX (confectioners') sugar**

1   Prepare the cake: Adjust oven racks with the bottom rack in the lower third and the top rack in the top third of the oven so that all three pans will fit into the oven at once. Preheat the oven to slow (325°). Grease and flour one 8 x 2-inch, one 9 x 2-inch and one 12 x 1-inch heart shape or round cake pans. Set aside.

2   Cream the butter, 2 cups sugar and vanilla in a large mixing bowl until light and fluffly. Add eggs one at a time, beating after each addition. Combine flours on a sheet of waxed paper. Alternately beat in flour mixture with the milk beginning and ending with the flour.

3   Using a small mixing bowl and clean beaters, beat egg whites until foamy. Gradually beat in remaining ¼ cup sugar until soft, firm peaks form. Fold egg whites gently into butter-sugar mixture until no streaks of white remain. Pour batter proportionately between the 3 prepared pans. Bake in the preheated slow oven (325°) for 35 minutes for the 8-inch layer, 1 hour for the 9-inch layer and 1 hour 30 minutes for the 12-inch layer, or until a wooden pick inserted in the center comes out clean. Cool the cakes in the pans on wire racks for 10 minutes. Loosen the cakes around the edges with a thin metal spatula and invert onto racks to cool completely.

4   Prepare the Buttercream Frosting: Beat together butter, milk, extracts and 5¼ cups IOX (confectioners') sugar in a large bowl until smooth. Slowly beat in 5¼ cups additional IOX (confectioners') sugar until the frosting is good spreading consistency.

5   Place each cake layer on a serving plate. Spread sides and top with about one half of the Buttercream Frosting. Fill a pastry bag fitted with a decorative tip with remaining frosting. Decorate each cake as desired. Garnish cake with fresh flowers and ribbons if desired.

SITTING PRETTY

What could be more romantic than this dreamy "sweet-heart" table for the the bride and groom.

❖ LACE FLOWERS ❖

Average: For those with some experience in crafting.

We used yards and yards of lace to drape the table and chairs. Tuck small sprigs of dried flowers among the roses in the table swags.

NOTE: For lace roses, you'll need several yards of lace, sewing thread to match, straight pins or staple gun.

1 *Cutting:* For small roses, cut 5"-wide strips of lace 12"-14" long. Fold a strip in half lengthwise and sew a gathering row along the matching edges.

2 *Rolling:* Slightly draw up the gathering row. Roll the lace tightly to form the rose center, securing the bottom edges with small stitches. Continue to roll the lace, but less closely, for wider petals, adjusting the gathering as needed. Fasten the base of each petal as you go. You can also turn the top folded edge downward like a rose petal.

3 *Leaves:* Fold a 2^1/$_2$" x 5" piece of lace in half to make a square. Bring each end of the fold downward to form a point with the two folds meeting at the vertical center. Sew a gathering row across the two lower edges. Pull up the gathers and fasten the thread end, letting the pointed end "cup" into a leaf shape.

❖ TOPIARY PLACE MARKER ❖

Average: For those with some experience in crafting.

MATERIALS
- ☐ **3" terra cotta pot**
- ☐ **¹/₂"-wide satin ribbon to make roses and to wrap the stem**
- ☐ **round cotton doily about 18" wide**
- ☐ **¹/₈"-wide satin ribbon for bows**
- ☐ **3"-dia. styrofoam ball**
- ☐ **scraps of tulle or tissue**
- ☐ **plaster of Paris**
- ☐ **craft glue**
- ☐ **pencil**

DIRECTIONS

1 *Stem:* Sharpen the pencil. Glue one end of ribbon below the point. Wrap the pencil with the ribbon and glue the other end. Press pointed end into the center of the foam ball.

2 *Roses:* Make 80 to 100 ribbon roses as instructed on page 61. Pin them to the ball.

3 *Pot:* Fill the pot with prepared plaster. Before it hardens, set the pencil, straight up, into the center of the pot. Support the pencil until it can stand alone when the plaster hardens.

4 *Finishing:* Set the pot in the center of the doily. Bring up the edges and tie a narrow ribbon around them to make a ruffle. Fill the rim of the pot with tulle. Tie narrow ribbon bows around the stem as shown. Rest the place card against the stem.

❖

PAINTED POT PLACE MARKERS

Easy: Achievable by anyone.

Wedding place markers need not be plain old white cards. Make something truly unique that will be a lasting souvenir for the family and guests. With these flower-filled pots, you won't need costly flower arrangements for the table.

MATERIALS
- ☐ **small terra cotta pot**
- ☐ **acrylic paints**

DIRECTIONS

1 Decorate pots by painting freehand with acrylic paints. If you prefer, stencil a design on the pots.

2 Paint each guest's name on a pot and fill with flowers.

Left: Topiary Place Marker; below: Painted Pot Place Marker

A gift of sweets is a time-honored tradition at special celebrations especially weddings. Simply place a handful of sugar-coated almonds into the center of a plate-sized circle of tulle. Gather up into bundles and tie up with satin cord or ribbon in colors to complement the table setting.

Above left: Rose Place Markers
Below: How to make bread dough roses

❖ ROSE PLACE MARKER ❖

Average: For those with some experience in crafting.

To make about 50 roses

MATERIALS
- ☐ **eight slices white bread**
- ☐ **clear-drying craft glue**
- ☐ **sieve**
- ☐ **fresh or dried rose leaf**
- ☐ **small scissors**
- ☐ **place card**
- ☐ **acrylic paints, or silver or gold spray paint**

DIRECTIONS

1   Cut crusts from bread. Crumble bread between fingers. Set aside crumbs to dry out a little. Push crumbs through a sieve until very fine.

2   Mix crumbs with enough glue to make a sticky mass. Knead this mixture until it becomes dough-like. This takes a few minutes so be patient and keep working at it!

3   To make a rose, form a bullet shape with a tiny piece of dough. Set this aside for the center. Take another tiny piece of dough and flatten it into an oval shape. Stretch the oval into a petal shape (Fig. 1).

4   Fold petal around center of rose one side at a time, with center protruding a little below petal and sides overlapping (Fig. 2).

5   Make a slightly wider petal and wrap it around center (Fig. 3). Build up rose in this way, adding a slightly larger petal each time (Figs. 4 and 5).

6   Stretch upper edges of last few petals to curve them outwards (Fig. 6).

7   To make leaves, roll out dough into an elongated shape then flatten it out. Taper both ends. Press dough on underside of rose leaf to make an impression of the veins. Being careful not to smudge veins, cut serrations along sides with small scissors and bend leaves into shape. Make as many roses as desired and set aside to dry.

8   Mold a ball of dough about the size of a walnut for the place maker base. Flatten underside so it sits properly. Cut a slit into top of base, at a slight angle, using a place card. Make sure card sits securely at desired angle, then put base aside to dry.

9   Attach roses and leaves to front and sides of base with craft glue.

10 Paint individual roses with acrylic colours or spray entire arrangement with silver or gold paint.

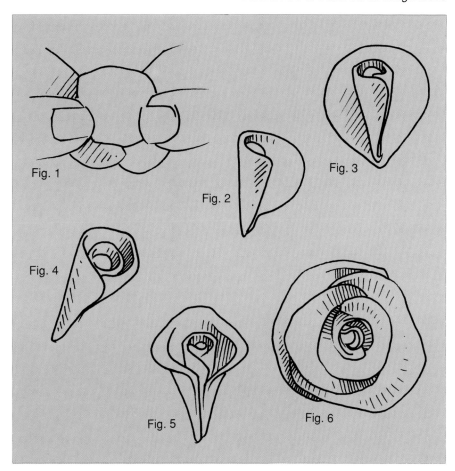

Fig. 1

Fig. 2

Fig. 3

Fig. 4

Fig. 5

Fig. 6

AL FRESCO LUNCH

Spread the joyous spirit by moving the lunch party into the garden where our alfresco dishes make entertaining a breeze.

❖

SEAFOOD SALAD WITH APRICOT DRESSING

Makes 10 servings.

- ☐ ³/₄ cup apricot nectar
- ☐ 2 tablespoons vegetable oil
- ☐ 1 tablespoon white wine vinegar
- ☐ 1 tablespoon lemon juice
- ☐ 1 tablespoon firmly packed brown sugar
- ☐ 2 pounds nectarines, sliced
- ☐ 1 pound fresh or frozen (thawed) lobster meat
- ☐ 1 pound medium-size, shelled, deveined and cooked shrimp
- ☐ 3 avocados, peeled, pitted and sliced
- ☐ 1 bunch watercress, stemed
- ☐ 6 green onions, finely chopped

1   Combine apricot nectar, vinegar, lemon juice, oil and brown sugar in a jar with a tight fitting lid. Refrigerate until ready to toss with salad.

2   Combine nectarines, lobster, shrimp, avocados, watercress and onions in a large bowl. Shake dressing well and pour over. Toss together until well combined.

❖

VEAL WITH SPICY FRUIT SAUCE

Try a mixture of brandy and apple juice or just apple juice .

Makes 10 servings.

VEAL
- ☐ 1 leek, washed thoroughly and sliced
- ☐ 1 carrot, pared and sliced
- ☐ 1 stalk celery, sliced
- ☐ 3¹/₂ pounds veal rolled rump roast
- ☐ 1 can (13¹/₂ ounces) chicken broth
- ☐ 1 tablespoon apple jelly
- ☐ 1 cup currants
- ☐ 1 tablespoon apple brandy

SAUCE
- ☐ 2 tablespoons butter or margarine
- ☐ 2 tablespoons flour
- ☐ 2 tablespoons apple jelly
- ☐ ¹/₄ cup apple brandy
- ☐ 2 teaspoons chopped crystallized ginger
- ☐ ¹/₄ cup heavy cream

1   Preheat oven to 350°.

2   To Prepare Veal: Combine leek, carrot and celery in a small shallow, open roasting pan. Place meat on top of vegetables and pour chicken broth over. Cover and roast in the preheated oven (350°) for 1 hour basting frequently with pan juices.

3   Remove the roast from the oven and raise the oven temperature to 400°. Uncover the roast and brush with the melted apple jelly.

4   Return the meat to the oven and roast for 30 minutes.

5   Meanwhile, combine currants and 1 tablespoon apple brandy in a small bowl. Let stand for 10 to 15 minutes.

6   Remove roast from oven; strain cooking liquid and reserve. Discard vegetables.

7   To Prepare Spicy Fruit Sauce: Melt butter in a medium-sized saucepan over medium-low heat. Add flour and cook, stirring constantly, 3 to 5 minutes or until thickened and bubbly. Gradually whisk in reserved liquid, 2 tablespoons apple jelly, ¹/₄ cup apple brandy and ginger. Bring to a boil over high heat, reduce heat to low and simmer until the sauce thickens slightly. Gradually whisk in the cream, whisking constantly. Stir in the currants and simmer for 1 to 2 minutes.

8   Slice meat and place on a warm platter. Spoon the sauce over.

Clockwise from top left: Harlequin Salad with Strawberry Dressing; Hot Potato Salad; Cassata Cake; Sweetheart Gateau; Veal with Spicy Fruit Sauce, Baby Beets, Snow Peas and Orange Salad; Chicken Roll with Pesto Sauce; Seafood Salad with Apricot Dressing

❖ CHICKEN ROLL WITH ❖
PESTO SAUCE

Makes 10 servings.
- [ ] **6¹/₂ pound capon or oven stuffer, boned**
- [ ] **¹/₂ teaspoon ground black pepper**
- [ ] **3 slices whole wheat bread, crusts trimmed away**
- [ ] **1 tablespoon sour cream**
- [ ] **2 tablespoons chopped fresh basil**
- [ ] **3 thin slices baked ham**
- [ ] **1 medium-size sweet red pepper, halved, cored, seeded, and cut into 3 x ¹/₄-inch strips**
- [ ] **2 ounces pepperoni, thinly sliced (about ¹/₄ cup)**
- [ ] **6 pimiento stuffed olives, sliced**
- [ ] **4 flat anchovy fillets**
- [ ] **1 hard cooked egg, peeled and sliced**
- [ ] **2 tablespoons butter or margarine, softened**
- [ ] **1 teaspoon leaf basil, crumbled**

PESTO SAUCE
- [ ] **¹/₂ cup firmly packed fresh basil leaves**
- [ ] **2 tablespoons pine nuts, toasted**
- [ ] **2 cloves garlic, crushed**
- [ ] **¹/₂ cup grated Parmesan cheese**
- [ ] **6 tablespoons olive oil**

1 Preheat the oven to moderate (350°).
2 Prepare the Chicken Roll: Cut capon through back, removing backbone, but

Below: Harlequin Salad with Strawberry Dressing; opposite from top:
Sweetheart Gateau; Cassata Cake

not cutting in half. Lay capon, skinside down on a work surface and with a boning knife, cut under the rib cage, removing breastbone and rib cage. Scrape flesh away from the thigh bone, then separate thigh bone from leg bone at joint, remove thigh bone from both sides. Cut wings at joint where they join to the body. Save for another use. Pound the capon lightly with a meat mallet to flatten slightly and evenly all over to a thickness of about ³/₄-inch. Sprinkle with pepper.
3 Place bread slices over center of capon. Spread bread with sour cream and sprinkle with basil. Top with ham, red pepper, pepperoni, olives and anchovy. Arrange egg slices overlapping slightly down the center of the chicken.
4 Starting at short side, roll chicken up, tucking in ingredients that might squeeze out. If possible, gently pull the skin to cover all the meat and fasten together with wooden picks. Tie the roll secure with string at 2¹/₂-inch intervals, set aside. Rub with butter and sprinkle with basil.
5 Place the roll seam-side down, on a rack in a roasting pan.
6 Bake in the preheated moderate oven (350°) for 1 to 1¹/₂ hours or until tender.
7 Meanwhile, prepare the Pesto Sauce: Combine the basil, pine nuts, garlic and Parmesan cheese in the container of an electric food processor or blender. Whirl at high speed until blended. With the motor still running, slowly pour the olive oil through the feed tube and whirl until puréed.
8 Cool roll slightly. Remove to a serving platter. Cover securely with foil and refrigerate overnight.
9 To serve, cut into slices and serve with pesto sauce.

❖ BABY BEETS ❖
SNOW PEAS
AND ORANGE SALAD

To cut preparation time on serving day, prepare the Orange Dressing several days before, cover, and refrigerate. The snow peas can be cooked the day before, covered and refrigerated.
Makes 10 servings.
- [ ] **3 tablespoons vegetable oil**
- [ ] **1 tablespoon tarragon vinegar**
- [ ] **1 tablespoon orange juice**
- [ ] **1¹/₂ teaspoons sugar**
- [ ] **1 teaspoon grated orange zest (orange part of rind only)**
- [ ] **1 pound snow peas, trimmed and strings removed**
- [ ] **2 cans (16 ounces) whole beets**

1 Combine oil, vinegar, orange juice, sugar and orange zest in a jar with a tight fitting lid. Reserve.
2 Bring 2 cups of water in a large skillet or saucepan to boiling. Add snow peas and cook for 2 to 3 minutes or until

tender-crisp. Transfer peas to colander and refresh under cold running water. Drain thoroughly. Pat dry with paper toweling.
3 Arrange beets and snow peas in a shallow glass serving bowl. Pour dressing over and refrigerate until ready to serve.

❖ HOT POTATO SALAD ❖

Prepare the dressing, cook the eggs and slice the onions, pepper and celery the day before .
Makes 10 servings.
- [ ] **³/₄ cup sour cream**
- [ ] **3 tablespoons mayonnaise**
- [ ] **1 clove garlic, crushed**
- [ ] **2¹/₄ pounds small red potatoes, about 1–2-inches in diameter**
- [ ] **5 hard cooked eggs, peeled and quartered**
- [ ] **1 sweet red pepper, halved, cored, seeded and coarsely chopped**
- [ ] **2 stalks celery, thinly sliced**
- [ ] **2 onions, thinly sliced**
- [ ] **2 tablespoons capers, drained**
- [ ] **2 tablespoons chopped fresh basil**
- [ ] **freshly ground black pepper**

1 Combine sour cream, mayonnaise and garlic in a large bowl. Mix together until well blended. Cover and refrigerate.
2 Cook the potatoes in their skins in boiling water until just tender, for about 15 to 20 minutes; the centers should not be soft. Drain. Rinse briefly under cold running water; drain.
3 Add the potatoes, eggs red pepper, celery, onions, capers, basil and black pepper, to taste Toss together until well coated.

❖ HARLEQUIN SALAD WITH ❖
STRAWBERRY DRESSING

Makes 10 servings.
- [ ] **¹/₂ cup raw brown rice, cooked and cooled**
- [ ] **¹/₂ cup raw white rice, cooked and cooled**
- [ ] **¹/₂ cup raw wild rice, cooked and cooled**
- [ ] **1¹/₂ cups strawberries, hulled**
- [ ] **¹/₂ cup golden raisins**
- [ ] **¹/₂ cup pumpkin seeds**
- [ ] **3 tablespoons chopped fresh mint**
- [ ] **2 tablespoons chopped candied ginger**
- [ ] **2 tablespoons vegetable oil**
- [ ] **2 teaspoons honey**
- [ ] **1 teaspoon grated fresh ginger**
- [ ] **1 teaspoon lime juice**
- [ ] **1 clove garlic, crushed**

1 Combine cooked and cooled brown, white and wild rice in a large bowl. Slice ³/₄ cup strawberries and add to the rice. Add raisins, pumpkin seeds, mint and candied ginger; set aside.
2 In the container of an electric food processor or blender, combine remaining strawberries, oil, honey, ginger, lime juice and garlic; whirl at high speed until smooth.
3 Pour dressing over rice mixture. Toss together until well combined. Cover and refrigerate for several hours or until thoroughly chilled.

❖ SWEETHEART GATEAU ❖

Make the meringue layers for this special gateau up to a week in advance and store in an airtight container.

Makes 10 servings.
MERINGUE
- ☐ 6 egg whites
- ☐ 1/8 teaspoon cream of tartar
- ☐ 1 1/2 cups superfine sugar
- ☐ 3/4 cup ground hazelnuts (filberts)

FILLING
- ☐ 5 1/2 squares (1 ounce each) semisweet chocolate
- ☐ 1 1/4 cups heavy cream, whipped
- ☐ 1 pound (about 3 cups) raspberries
- ☐ IOX (confectioners') sugar

1   Preheat the oven to slow (200°). Line 1 large and 1 medium-size or small cookie sheet with parchment paper. Using an 8-inch heart shaped pan as a guide, draw 2 heart shaped outlines on the large piece of parchment and 1 on the small. Invert paper so markings are on the underside.

2   Prepare the Meringue: Beat together the egg whites and cream of tartar in a large mixing bowl until soft peaks form. Gradually beat in the sugar, 1 tablespoon at a time, until the mixture forms very stiff peaks. Fold in the hazelnuts.

3   To secure paper on sheet, dot underside of each paper corner with a dab of the meringue. Fill a pastry bag fitted with a large writing tip with the meringue. Holding the bag in a vertical position with the tube at least 1 1/2-inches above the heart, pipe the heart outline, beginning and ending at the indentation. Continue piping 1 row at a time, ending at the center. Use a small brush dipped in water to correct mistakes. Bake in the preheated slow oven (200°) for 1 hour 30 minutes or until firm. Turn oven off and let meringues stand overnight in the turned off oven. Loosen the meringues carefully with a small thin metal spatula; transfer to a wire rack to cool completely. Store in a tightly covered container in a dry place until ready to assemble.

4   Prepare the Filling: Melt the chocolate in the top of a double boiler set over hot, not boiling water, stirring occasionally until smooth.

5   Place one meringue heart on a serving platter and spread with half the chocolate mixture, half the cream and one third of the raspberries. Top with second heart and repeat the layering. Top with the third heart and remaining raspberries. Dust lightly with the IOX (confectioners') sugar.

❖ CASSATA CAKE ❖

Make the biscuit layer up to 1 week in advance and store in an airtight container. The filling can be made the day before and stored in the refrigerator.

Makes 10 servings.
BISCUIT LAYER
- ☐ 1 cup sifted all-purpose flour
- ☐ 1/2 cup (1 stick) unsalted butter or margarine, softened
- ☐ 3 tablespoons firmly packed light brown sugar
- ☐ 3 tablespoons finely chopped almonds

FILLING
- ☐ 1 1/4 cups chopped glace fruit
- ☐ 1 tablespoon Benedictine liqueur
- ☐ 2 ounces white chocolate
- ☐ 1/2 cup (1 stick) unsalted butter or margarine, softened
- ☐ 3/4 cup superfine sugar
- ☐ 2 eggs

TOPPING
- ☐ 1 cup cream
- ☐ 2 teaspoons Benedictine
- ☐ 1/2 cup chocolate chips, melted and cooled
- ☐ chocolate curls
- ☐ crystallized violets (optional)

1   Preheat the oven to hot (400°), Grease and wax paper line a 11 x 7 x 1 1/2-inch shallow baking pan. Set aside.

2   Prepare the Biscuit Layer: Combine flour and butter in a medium-size bowl. Using a pastry blender or 2 knives, cut butter until mixture resembles fine crumbs. Add brown sugar and almonds and work into a soft paste. Press mixture into prepared pan.

3   Bake in the preheated hot oven (400°) for 20 minutes or until golden brown. Cool the biscuit in the pan on a wire rack.

4   Prepare the Filling: Combine glacé fruit and Benedictine in a small bowl; cover and let stand for 1 hour. Meanwhile, melt the white chocolate in the top of a double boiler set over hot (not boiling) water. Remove from the heat and set aside to cool.

5   Beat the butter and sugar in a small bowl until creamy. Add eggs, one at a time, beating well after each addition. Stir in cooled white chocolate and fruit.

6   Turn out the cooled biscuit and remove the waxed paper. Place biscuit on a serving platter, spread chocolate fruit mixture over top and refrigerate for 2 hours.

7   Prepare the Topping: Beat together cream and Benedictine in a small bowl until stiff. Fold in chocolate; refrigerate.

8   Using a long thin serrated knife, slice biscuit in half lengthwise through the middle of the layer. Place one half of the biscuit cut side down on a serving plate and spread with half the chocolate cream mixture. Top with remaining biscuit half. Fill a pastry bag fitted with a decorative tip with the remaining chocolate cream mixture and pipe around the top edges of the cassata. Decorate with chocolate curls and crystalized violets if desired. Refrigerate until ready to serve.

BEAUTIFUL BRIDE

Follow our guide to look radiant on your wedding day.

Good health and clear skin make a beautiful bride. If you watch what you eat, exercise regularly and follow a beauty care routine for your skin, nails and hair, you will not only look fabulous at your wedding, but you will retain that glow.

For many women, the announcement of their engagement signals the start of a strict diet. Shedding a few pounds to look slim and beautiful in your wedding gown is fine, but diet sensibly. Planning a wedding puts a lot of pressure on the bride, and you'll need your strength for the months of preparation. Make sure you're getting the vitamins and nutrients you need to stay healthy. The last thing you want is to be slim, and totally exhausted on your wedding day. If you want to lose a lot of weight, consult a doctor about a weight-loss program.

Even though you'll be very busy with work, everyday details and wedding plans, don't neglect your regular exercise routine. An aerobics class, set of tennis or brisk after-work run can help reduce tension and burn off nervous energy. Try to get some aerobic exercise – for at least 30 minutes – three times a week.

If your skin tends to break out in times of stress, begin a skin care program as soon as you can. Many beauty experts recommend that women begin skin treatments at least three months before their weddings. Visit a

skin care specialist or dermatologist for advice before beginning any treatments. Facials are the best method for clearing the skin of impurities and blemishes. Even if you have good skin, you should try to have a facial twice, two weeks apart, about 2 to 6 weeks before the wedding.

Once your diet, exercise and skin care regimes are all in place, it's time to consider your hairstyle and make up for the wedding. Some women prefer a "come as you are" approach to beauty. Others may feel that their everyday look is not glamorous enough for a bride. Experiment

to find the look that's right for you.

Before you decide on a hairstyle, choose your bridal headpiece. Will you wear a wide-brimmed hat or a veil? A garland of flowers or a sparkling tiara? If possible, bring the headpiece with you when you visit your hair stylist. Discuss the look you want to achieve – soft and flowing, sleek and dramatic – and how it can work with your headpiece and gown. If you are planning a drastic change in your hairstyle, test it out before the wedding so there are no surprises on the big day. If you like, ask your stylist to come to your home on the morning of the wedding to be sure your hair looks perfect.

Make-up can be tricky and it's best to take some time to find a look that works for you. Color analysis is a good place to start, and you should think about this before you buy your gown. When you begin shopping for your gown, you'll discover there are many shades of white. The wrong one can make you look sallow or drained, the right one can make you look luminous.

Remember that you'll be dressed in white and you'll be photographed all day. Even if you never wear make-up, the least you'll need is blush, lip gloss and mascara to keep you from washing out in the photographs. If you're not a wizard with make-up, or if you think wedding day jitters will make you too frantic to do your own face, hire a make-up consultant to do your make-up on the day of the wedding. Your hair stylist or bridal salon can probably recommend someone.

Manicures and pedicures are the finishing touch where beauty is concerned. A pedicure can smooth rough spots on your feet, remove calluses and make your toes look pretty. A manicure includes buffing the nail surface, clipping dry cuticles and moisturizing the hands. You might also want to have artificial tips applied to some or all of your nails to give you a perfect "10".

Nail colour is a personal preference, but clear soft colours such as shell pink or pearl enamel are most popular and the most traditional. French manicures, where the nail plate is given a natural pink shade and the tips are accentuated with

white, have also become popular with brides. Buy your own, high-quality, nail color and keep it in your make-up case to repair any chips before the wedding.

In the flurry of activity surrounding a wedding it's sometimes difficult to take time to relax, but it's very important that you give yourself a "breather". Take an evening off, at the movies with your friends or at home on the couch with a good book. Sit in a whirlpool or sauna to clear your head.

A nightly bath scented with aromatic essential oils, such as lavender, is wonderfully relaxing. Chamomile also has a soothing effect and is good for ensuring sound sleep (try it the night before the wedding). Cold chamomile tea bags refresh tired eyes. Peppermint tea aids digestion and also relaxes the nervous system. For a real indulgence, treat yourself to a full body

massage or an afternoon at a spa or beauty salon.

You'll want to go out celebrating with friends, especially as the wedding draws near. Have fun, but take it easy. If you drink alcohol, do it in moderation.

The time before your wedding is likely to be one of the most emotional, exciting, frustrating and gratifying times of your life. It's the perfect time to make yourself feel a little bit special. Treat yourself well before your wedding and it will show. You'll be the most beautiful bride you can be.

❖

THE GLAMOROUS GARTER

Sweet and sexy, this garter is easy to make and it will delight any bride.

MATERIALS
- ☐ **1 yd. double-edged lace**
- ☐ **1 yd. ⁵⁄₈"-wide satin ribbon**
- ☐ **elastic to fit, above the knee**
- ☐ **ribbon roses (see page 61)**

DIRECTIONS
1 *Seaming:* Seam the cut ends of lace together to form a circle. Press the seam open and overcast or zigzag stitch the raw edges. Seam the ribbon the same way.
2 *Ribbon:* Pin the ribbon over the center of the lace, right sides up; edgestitch.
3 *Elastic:* Open the ribbon seam and insert the elastic. Stitch the elastic ends securely together. Close the ribbon seam by hand.
4 *Roses:* Make ribbon roses as instructed on page 61. Handsew them to the ribbon.

❖ **BLUE GARTERS** ❖
The custom of throwing the bride's blue garter to the male guests dates from the fourteenth century and mirrors the throwing of the bouquet. The blue colour symbolises purity, love and faithfulness.

B O W S
FOR THE VEIL

Trim a simple veil with one of these fabulous net bows or attach one to a comb for a lovely hair accessory.

All the bows are made from strips of double layers of net, cut slightly wider than their finished width. Fasten the two layers together by stitching ribbon, about $1/8$" wide, along the edges; then trim back the net to meet the ribbon if it's needed.

For the pink and cream bows, make around 10 loops of net, stitched into a pompon shape. Decorate with ribbon roses, glued on at random, or with streamers of narrow ribbon.

The cream bow shows how the ribbon that finishes the edges can be stitched down the centre of double-edged lace for a different effect.

The yellow bow has a rose, made from rolled (see page 49) and ribbon-trimmed net, as its center.

Photography by Alan Khan and Christopher Poulos

FLOWERS
FOR THE VEIL

For a sophisticated but very romantic look, trim a veil with these beautiful flowers made from silk organza.

MATERIALS
- [ ] **silk organza**
- [ ] **fabric stiffener (from a craft shop) or a solution of 1 part clear-drying glue and 12 parts tepid water**
- [ ] **tracing paper**
- [ ] **hair comb (optional)**

DIRECTIONS

1 *Stiffening:* Saturate the organza with the stiffening solution. Hang it up to dry, without wringing it. Smooth out the wrinkles as the fabric dries.

2 *Cutting:* Trace each of the two petal patterns on tracing paper. For each flower, cut about five small petals and twenty-five large ones.

> ### ❖ VEILS UNVEILED ❖
> Veils were originally designed to protect the bride from evil spirits and ensure a lucky marriage. Cautious grooms insisted that the veil be thrown back after the ceremony to ensure they had the right bride!

3 *Wrapping:* Beginning with the smaller petals, wrap them around each other, one at a time, at the narrow "neck". Overlap the edges and sew the ends together as you wrap.

4 *Shaping:* The central petals can be twisted into stamen if you like. On others, gently pull the petals on the bias grain to look like a flower.

5 *Comb:* Fasten the flowers to the comb and veil.

CROWNING
GLORY

*Pretty as a picture, these two beautiful bridesmaids are
wearing wreaths of fresh flowers in their hair. Make them
with fresh flowers like these, or use ribbon roses to
make a colorful, long-lasting wreath.*

❖ RIBBON-ROSE WREATH ❖

MATERIALS

- ☐ ¹/₂ yd. ³/₈"-wide satin ribbon for each rose
- ☐ ¹/₂ yd. ¹/₈"-wide satin ribbon for each bow
- ☐ extra thick pipe cleaners, from craft stores
- ☐ 1 yd. ³/₄"-wide ribbon for the foundation wreath

DIRECTIONS

1   *Foundation Wreath:* Twist enough pipe cleaners together to go around head. Twist a second strand of pipe cleaners around the first for added strength. Wind the ³/₄" ribbon around the wreath to cover the pipe cleaners and glue the ribbon ends securely in place.

2   *Roses:* Make ribbon roses as shown in the box at the right. Mix colors of your choice and make enough (about 30) to cover the base generously.

❖ WEDDING WAYS ❖

Some African tribes bind together the wrists of the bride and groom with braided grass.

In Czechoslovakia, rural brides wear rosemary wreaths woven for them on the eve of their wedding.

In Germany, the bride and groom hold candles trimmed with flowers and ribbons.

Greek brides carry a lump of sugar in their gloves for sweetness in married life.

In India, the groom's brother sprinkles flower petals on the bridal couple.

❖ HOW TO MAKE RIBBON ROSES ❖

Note: The length of the ribbon determines the size of the rose.

1   Roll one end of ribbon about six times to form a tight tube. Sew a few stitches at base to secure it (Fig. A).

2   To form a petal, fold the top edge of the ribbon down towards you so that it lies parallel to the tube and the folded edge is at a 45° angle (Fig. A).

3   Pivoting the lower edge, roll the central tube across the fold, loosely at the top and tightly at the base (Figs. B and C). Stitch the lower edge.

4   Repeat Steps 2 and 3, shaping the petals as you go (Fig. D) until it looks like a rose. Tight winding forms a bud while loose winding forms a rose.

5   Trim off any extra ribbon, turn under the raw end and stitch it to the base of the flower.

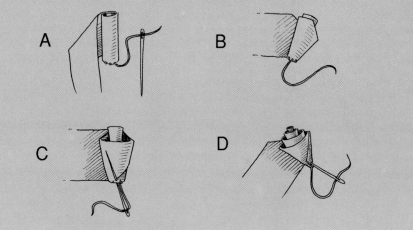

Ribbon Rose Circlet

❖
SIMPLE FRESH FLOWER WREATH

It is quite easy to make a headband or wreath from real flowers. Make a base for the flowers as instructed in Ribbon Rose Wreath, above. Place flower onto wreath laying stem against wreath. Wind ¹/₂" wired ribbon around wreath and stem until stem is covered. Lay next flower head over wrapped stem and wind its stem. Cover complete wreath with flowers working in only one direction. Finish off ribbon with stitching or concealed pin.

BRAIDED BEAUTY

You've chosen your dress and veil, and now it's time to decide on the perfect hairstyle to complement the total look. We selected this beautiful and very unusual braided style for the bride with long, straight hair. It will look best worn with a simple veil. These step-by-step pictures will serve as a guide for your hairdresser.

STEP 1
Brush hair carefully to remove all tangles before you begin. Part hair through the center or natural parting. Form a 'V' section on one side of the part.

STEP 2
Divide the "V" section into two. Tie ribbon to back section. Using "figure eight" method, wrap ribbon over and under first section and then over and under second section.

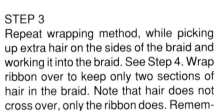

STEP 3
Repeat wrapping method, while picking up extra hair on the sides of the braid and working it into the braid. See Step 4. Wrap ribbon over to keep only two sections of hair in the braid. Note that hair does not cross over, only the ribbon does. Remember to pick up a new section of hair every time you wrap ribbon over.

STEP 4
Before repeating STEP 3, remove a fine strand of hair from the middle of the second section before ribbon wraps over. Use end of comb to pick up this strand.

STEP 5
Place hair strand onto first section and wrap the ribbon over it to secure. This creates loops of hair down the center of the braid.

STEP 6
Repeat the braiding method through to the end of the hair, distributing the hair evenly around the crown. As braids pass nape of neck, pick up hair from crown only.

STEP 7
Loop ribbon into a half knot to finish off.

STEP 8
Repeat for other side and tie together.

STEP 9
Lift the strands lying over center of ribbons with a tail comb to form loops.

STEP 10
Finish off with bows and miniature roses. Cut off loose end of ribbon at the top and tuck it into the braid.

LOVE IN

Flowers are the language of love, so let them burst forth at your wedding! Beautiful flower arrangements can transform the plainest church or reception venue into a fantasy of color and scent.

When choosing flowers, think in terms of your overall color scheme, the bridal party gowns and the ceremony and reception venues. Select any flowers you like, but remember that some are only available in season.

Consult with a florist when you have confirmed the venues and selected the bridesmaids' gowns. The florist should be able to show you photographs of his or her work and will provide you with an estimated cost for the flowers you choose. If possible, provide the florist with a fabric swatch from the bridesmaids' dresses.

Flowers for the bridal party include bouquets or nosegays for the bridesmaids and flowergirls (the florist can also prepare hair combs or garlands for the attendants), boutonnieres for the groom, his attendants and the fathers, and corsages for the mothers of the bride and groom. Most important, of course, is the bridal bouquet.

Think of the bridal bouquet as an accessory to complement your gown. The bridal bouquet is usually white, but you might like to add a few colored flowers for interest. Be sure you include some sweet-smelling flowers, so the fragrance follows you up the aisle.

Orange blossoms have been traditional for bridal bouquets since the days of the Crusades. Because the orange tree is ever-green, its blossoms were said to symbolize everlasting love.

An armful of long-stemmed flowers can also make a beautiful bridal bouquet, or, for a touch of

BLOOM

tradition, carry a copy of your mother's or grandmother's bouquet. A tight bouquet is the most suitable style for a period gown, while a trailing bouquet balances the lines of a dress with a long train.

For the groom, lily-of-the-valley is the traditional choice, however, the fragile flower has been know to wilt in the heat of the moment. Stephanotis is a fine substitute, as is a white rose.

For the ceremony, you will require flowers for the altar and the aisle. Check with your clergyman before ordering flowers for the ceremony, the church may provide its own flowers or vases. The florist can usually use the reception table arrangements as aisle flowers.

Flowers for the reception vary by taste and budget, but you will probably want an arrangement for each table. White is often the predominant color, but you may use any colors you like. Delicate pink, peach or yellow flowers blend beautifully with pastel bridesmaids' gowns. For an autumn or winter wedding, try rich red roses or purple irises.

Important tip! Arrange for the florist to show you a sample table arrangement at least a week before the wedding so you can check the colors and design before the big day.

Many brides dream of a garden wedding. If it is between seasons, you can heighten the impact of color and scent by bringing in potted plants or shrubs.

If your wedding will take place at home, bring the garden indoors with flowering shrubs. Frame the doorways of the house with flowers.

After the wedding, dry your own flowers as a souvenir of the day (see page 71).

THE LANGUAGE OF
FLOWERS

Traditionally, different flowers have been thought to carry various meanings. The ancient Greeks favored lilies for innocence while Roman brides wore garlands of flowers and herbs. In Germany, myrtle symbolises purity and fertility.

FLOWERS AND THEIR MEANINGS

acacia	secret love
camellia	excellence
carnation	distinction
forget-me-not	true love
daisy	innocence
gardenia	joy
honeysuckle	devotion
ivy	marriage, fidelity
lily	purity
lily-of-the-valley	happiness
myrtle	purity and fertility
orange blossom	loveliness and happiness
pansy	shyness
rose	love
rosemary	remembrance and commitment

FLORAL CALENDAR

Use this seasonal guide to help you choose flowers at their best for your bouquet.

❖

SPRING

Apple blossom, azalea, blue-bell, camellia, clematis, daffodil, daisy, forget-me-not, hyacinth, jasmine, lily-of-the-valley, lilac, mimosa, narcissus, primrose, rhododendron, tulip.

❖

SUMMER

Azalea, alstroemeria, aster, daisy, delphinium, fuchsia, golden rod, geranium, gladiola, hydrangea, heather, hollyhock, lupin, lily-of-the-valley, lilac, marigold, shasta daisy, phlox, peony, rhododendron, sweetpea, sweet William, tiger lily.

❖

AUTUMN

Alstroemeria, amaryllis, daisy, jasmine, snowdrop.

❖

ALL YEAR ROUND

Baby's breath, bouvardia, carnation, chrysanthemum, freesia, gladiola, iris, lily, orchid, rose, stephanotis.

❖ A FAMILY HEIRLOOM ❖

Most brides want to keep their wedding gowns as a lasting memento and perhaps even to pass it on to their own daughters. To store your gown safely, fold it in layers of acid-free tissue paper and place it in a large box. If you want to be even more careful you can then wrap the box in a black cotton bag. Lay the box flat and store it in a cool, dry place. Many dry-cleaners will clean and package your gown for long-term storage.

F R A G R A N T
F L O W E R S

Some simple guidelines for making bouquets and garlands.

❖ A SIMPLE NOSEGAY ❖

Pefect for a bridesmaid.

Easy: Achievable by anyone.

MATERIALS
- [ ] **Four or more varieties of flowers, such as rosebuds, cornflowers. baby's breath, pansies**
- [ ] **evergreen foliage**
- [ ] **floral wire**
- [ ] **green floral tape**
- [ ] **½-inch-wide satin ribbon**

DIRECTIONS

1 Gather a small bunch of flowers, using one of each variety (Fig. A). Wire them together.

2 Continue adding one flower or evergreen leaf at a time, turning the nosegay in your hand and wiring the flowers to sit at an angle (Fig. A). When the nosegay is complete, wind green floral tape around the stems, bending them slightly (Fig. B). Stretch the tape as you wind it so it clings to the stems. Decorate the finished nosegay with bows and streamers of satin ribbon.

The romance of a beautiful bouquet

Photography by Alan Khan and Christopher Poulos

❖ FLOWERS IN HER HAIR ❖

Choose flowers that complement the bouquet and dress, and are the right size for the wearer.

Easy: Achievable by anyone.

MATERIALS
- [ ] **Flowers, four or more varieties**
- [ ] **floral wire**
- [ ] **medium gauge wire (optional)**
- [ ] **floral tape**
- [ ] **½-inch wide ribbon (optional)**

DIRECTIONS

1 Wire each flower individually with floral wire, covering the stems with floral tape then joining them together. Start with just a couple of stems positioned so that one side will lie flat against the head (Fig. C).

2 To make a headband, either make a base of medium-gauge wire covered with floral tape and wire flowers around it, or bind individually wired flowers together without a base. Finish both ends of the headband with tapering blossoms pointing to the back (Fig. D). Curve the completed headband to fit and hold it in place with bobby pins or ribbons (Fig. E).

3 Make a circlet in the same way as the headband, wiring the flowers to a prepared wire base (Fig. F) or making a circle of wired flowers (Fig G).

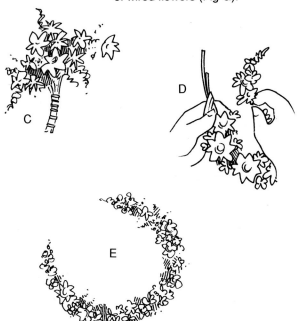

❖ BEAUTIFUL BOUQUETS ❖

Here are tips for making a formal bouquet and an informal cascade of flowers.
Average: For those with some experience in flower arranging.

MATERIALS

- [ ] **flowers and buds: several varieties, including baby's breath**
- [ ] **evergreen foliage (we used ferns and ivy for the informal bouquet, just ferns for the formal)**
- [ ] **floral wire**
- [ ] **green floral tape**
- [ ] **your choice of ribbon**

DIRECTIONS

1   An informal, loose bouquet (inset), should be wired as little as possible. Lay the flowers with the longer and stronger stems at the back and, using these as your base, build up the bouquet, tapering the top and edges. Bind the stems together carefully with floral tape to secure the bouquet. To form a trail of flowers to hang from the bouquet, begin with a small flower or bud and gradually build up the shape (Fig. H). Position the trail and wire it into place.

2   To form a tighter bouquet, each bloom must be wired individually, covered with floral tape and then bound together when a pleasing shape is achieved. Join a few flowers together by twisting the stems (Fig. I). Make three or four sprays and then join them together (Fig. J). Position the largest flowers in the center and the smaller ones at the sides, tapering to a point if desired. Bend the wires as you go so that the bouquet arches gracefully (Fig. K). Bind the stems with floral tape and trim with bows or ribbons.

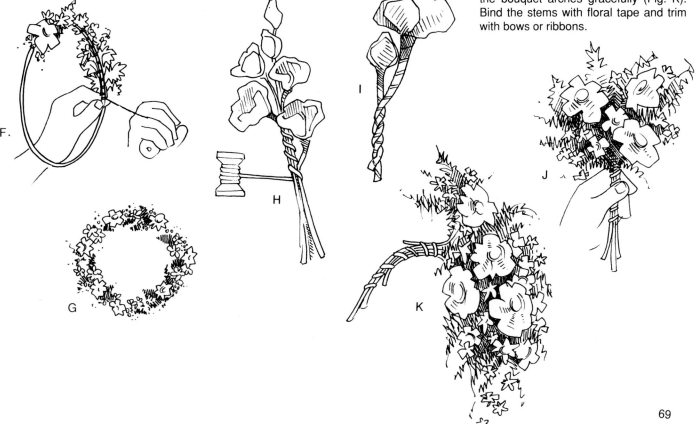

EVERLASTING MEMORIES

When the wedding is long past, the happy couple can continue to enjoy these reminders of that special day.

❖

SILK-COVERED PHOTO ALBUM

Average: For those with some experience in crafting.

MATERIALS
- ☐ **photo album**
- ☐ **silk taffeta**
- ☐ **synthetic batting**
- ☐ **fusible interfacing**
- ☐ **embroidery floss**

DIRECTIONS

1 *Cutting:* Measure the total width (front, spine and back) of the album when it is closed and add 8" for the two flaps. Measure the length (top to bottom) of the cover and add 1" for seams. In this length and width, cut two pieces of silk and one piece of fusible interfacing. Also cut two $5^1/_2$" x 20 " silk strips for the tie.

2 *Interfacing:* Fuse interfacing to one silk piece for the cover (the other silk piece is the lining).

3 *Embroidery:* Turning under a 4"-wide flap, lightly mark the embroidery placement so it will center on the front cover. Turn the flap out again and embroider the rose buds (see page 37).

4 *Batting:* Smooth batting over the back of the cover and baste it $^3/_8$" from the edges. Trim off batting edges $^1/_8$" from the basting.

5 *Seaming:* Pin the lining over the cover, right sides together. Stitch $^3/_8$" from the four edges, leaving an opening for turning. Turn and press; close the opening by hand.

6 *Flaps:* Center the notebook over the lining side of the cover. Turn in each flap; close the book and pin the top and bottom edge of each flap to the front or back cover. Remove the book, then sew the flap edges in place with small slipstitches.

7 *Ties:* Fold each tie strip in half (to $2^3/_4$" x 20"), right sides together, and seam the raw edges, leaving a small opening for turning. Turn and press them. Sew one end of each tie to the center of one of the front edges of the cover. Close the cover and tie a bow.

This wonderful bridal wreath has been made from the dried flowers of the wedding bouquet. To preserve the flowers, spread them on a flat tray and dry them overnight in a very slow oven (200°). They are dried when they feel papery to the touch. With quick-drying craft glue, attach the flowers to the wreath base, adding ribbons if you wish. Attach a wire loop to the back for hanging.

To dry a complete bridal bouquet without losing its shape, use silica gel or another packaged floral preservative and follow the manufacturer's directions.

Some florists and specialty shops can recreate your bouquet or table arrangements with silk flowers for a lasting momento.

KEEPING A
RECORD

Memories may fade but photographs can be treasured long after the wedding. Plan your photographs or video carefully to capture this once-in-a-lifetime occasion.

Wedding photography is an art form requiring skill and careful planning – don't depend on candid shots taken by well-wishing friends and family to fill your wedding album. Choose a reliable and imaginative wedding photographer. If you know somebody with proven photographic skills and good quality camera equipment, invite him or her to be the official photographer for the day. If not, seek the expertise of a professional photographer.

When you choose a photographer it is most important that you feel comfortable and happy with both the photographer and his or her style. You're sure to be tense on your wedding day, but a good photographer can help you relax and look your best.

Begin "shopping around" for the right photographer as early as possible. Visit several studios, ask to see sample wedding albums and compare the quality of work. Spend some time with the photographer before the wedding and discuss the mood you wish to capture in your photographs. If you like, ask for candid shots for your album. Invite the photographer to the wedding venue to see the surroundings and lighting.

Traditionally, photographs are taken at the bride's house or bride's room before the ceremony, in front of the church or wedding site, at the signing of

Remember the happiest day of your life

the register and when the wedding party emerges from the ceremony. If you plan to take photographs during the ceremony ask your clergyman for permission. Some clergymen will not permit photography during the ceremony, others will simply not allow the photographer to use a flash attachment.

After the ceremony, the bridal couple, their attendants and immediate family gather for group photographs and portraits. Although it is considered bad luck for the groom to see the bride before the ceremony many couples opt to take most of their

portraits beforehand so they are free to mingle and enjoy the festivities after the ceremony.

At the reception, the photographer will take pictures of the bridal party seated at their table, the cake, the bride and her father dancing, the groom and his mother dancing, the musicians, the bride and groom cutting the cake, the bride tossing the bouquet, the newlyweds leaving the reception and guests waving good-bye. You may also request a photo of each table of guests.

The ultimate record of a wedding is a videotape through which you can re-live the whole event.

If you plan to use a professional video film maker, ask for recommendations from your photographer or caterer. Be sure to see a demonstration tape before you contract for a video. Book well in advance and make a list of the events you would like to be filmed. Be forewarned, making a good quality video involves microphones and powerful lighting equipment. Sometimes this may intrude on the festivities.

Introduce the video film maker to your wedding director, caterer or band leader so he or she is aware of the program for the reception. Feel confident and know what to expect so that picture-taking on the big day goes smoothly.

SIMPLE
CELEBRATION

Imagination is the most essential ingredient when preparing food for a wedding reception. This menu, which serves 25, is a celebration for the tastebuds.

❖ MINIATURE ❖
OPEN FACE SANDWICHES

These miniature open face sandwiches make wonderful finger food. To add interest and variety, use different types of bread such as rye and pumpernickel, flavored butters and different varieties of lettuce.

Makes 20 sandwiches.

- ☐ **1 large French bread (baguette)**
- ☐ **butter or margarine, softened**
- ☐ **Topping: see list below**

1   Slice French bread and cut into bite size desired shapes. Thinly spread one side of each slice with butter. Place on a serving tray, cover with plastic wrap and refrigerate.
2   Just before serving, arrange desired topping on each slice.

❖ TASTY TOPPINGS ❖

- ☐ cucumber slices with sour cream and caviar
- ☐ lettuce with smoked chicken, cherry tomatoes and coriander
- ☐ smoked salmon with camembert slices, avocado and lemon
- ☐ lettuce with Stilton and asparagus
- ☐ lettuce with sliced hard-cooked eggs and tomatoes
- ☐ rare roast beef with horseradish and watercress sprigs
- ☐ asparagus with mayonnaise and chopped hard-cooked egg
- ☐ lettuce with sour cream, oysters and chives
- ☐ bibb lettuce with large cooked shrimp and herbed mayonnaise

❖ MARINATED ❖
CHICKEN STRIPS

These tasty chicken strips are prepared and left to marinate overnight.

Makes 25 servings.

- ☐ **25 3-inch wooden toothpicks**
- ☐ **³/₄ cup hoisin sauce**
- ☐ **¹/₄ cup pineapple juice**
- ☐ **3 tablespoons teriyaki sauce**
- ☐ **2 tablespoons vegetable oil**
- ☐ **2 teaspoons grated fresh ginger**
- ☐ **1¹/₂ pounds skinless, boneless, chicken breast halves, flattened slightly and cut into 2 x 1-inch strips**

1   Submerge wooden toothpicks in a pan of water and soak for 2 to 4 hours or overnight.
2   Combine hoisin sauce, pineapple juice, teriyaki sauce, oil and ginger in a medium size bowl. Add chicken and stir to coat. Cover and refrigerate for 2 to 4 hours or overnight.
3   Preheat the broiler according to the manufacturer's directions.
4   Meanwhile, thread two pieces of chicken onto each of the soaked toothpicks.
5   Broil or grill the chicken on a lightly oiled broiler pan rack or grill rack 4-inches from the heat, basting frequently with the marinade, for 6 to 8 minutes turning occasionally.
Note: Hoisin sauce may be obtained in the Oriental foods section of the supermarket or Oriental specialty food shops.

❖ ASPARAGUS WITH ❖
PROSCIUTTO HAM

The asparagus may be blanched the day before and wrapped with ham. Cover with plastic food wrap and refrigerate. The Vinaigrette Dressing may also be prepared several days in advance and refrigerated.

Makes 25 servings.

VINIAGRETTE DRESSING
- ☐ **¹/₂ cup olive oil**
- ☐ **¹/₄ cup tarragon vinegar**
- ☐ **1 tablespoon whole grain mustard**
- ☐ **freshly ground black pepper**
- ☐ **1¹/₂ pounds fresh asparagus, tough stalks trimmed**
- ☐ **9 slices prosciutto ham**

1   Combine oil, vinegar, mustard and pepper in a screw top jar with a tight fitting lid. Shake well to blend mixture.
2   Bring 1 quart of water in a large skillet or Dutch oven to boiling. Add the asparagus. Cook for 3 to 5 minutes or until tender crisp. Drain in colander and rinse thoroughly under cold running water, drain well.
3   Cut the prosciutto into three lengthwise strips. Wrap a strip of prosciutto around each asparagus spear.
4   Arrange wrapped asparagus spears on a serving platter and pour over dressing.

❖ MINI QUICHES ❖

Our delicate but filling recipes look inviting and attractive but are just a mouthful – they're perfect for eating and socializing at the same time! To save time, prepare the day before serving, refrigerate and allow to come to room temperature before serving.

Makes 24 quiches.

PASTRY CUPS
- ☐ **2 sheets (1 package 17¹/₄ ounces) prepared puff pastry**
- ☐ **Carrot and Feta Cheese Filling: (recipe follows)**
- ☐ **Broccoli and Lemon Filling : (recipe follows)**
- ☐ **French Onion Filling: (recipe follows)**

1   Preheat the oven to moderate (350°). Lightly grease two mini-muffin cup pans; set aside.
2   Prepare the Pastry Cups: Unfold the sheets of puff pastry. While working, keep the unused puff pastry covered with a damp towel to prevent drying out. Using a 2¹/₂-inch round biscuit or plain cookie cut-

ter, cut the pastry into rounds. Place 1 round in each cup, filling smoothly in bottom and around the inside. Roll under edges with fingers to make a smooth, stand-up edge. Crimp to make a decorative edge. Fill pastry cups with desired filling.

3   Bake in the preheated moderate oven (350°) for 15 minutes or until pastry is golden brown. Remove from the oven. Let stand for 5 minutes. Carefully remove the cups from the pan to a wire rack. Serve warm or at room temperature.

❖ SMOKED SALMON ❖
AND CRAB ROLLS

Makes 20 rolls.

- ☐ **1 can (8 ounces) crabmeat, drained**
- ☐ **¹/₂ cup ricotta cheese**
- ☐ **2 tablespoons capers, drained and chopped**
- ☐ **2 tablespoons mayonnaise**
- ☐ **2 teaspoons lemon juice**
- ☐ **freshly ground black pepper**
- ☐ **liquid red pepper seasoning, to taste**

- ☐ **¹/₂ pound thinly sliced smoked salmon**
- ☐ **1 bunch fresh dill, stemmed and finely chopped**
- ☐ **lemon slices**

1   Pick over crabmeat to remove any cartilage or pieces of shell.

2   Combine crabmeat, ricotta cheese, capers, mayonnaise, lemon juice, black pepper and liquid red pepper seasoning in a small bowl. Mix together until well combined.

3   Spread equal amounts of the crab mixture onto each slice of salmon. Roll up from the short side and cut into 1-inch lengths; secure each roll firmly with a wooden pick.

4   Lightly brush end of each roll with water and dip into chopped dill.

5   Cover with plastic wrap and refrigerate until ready to serve.

6   Serve with lemon slices.

❖ TROPICAL SHRIMP ❖

Makes 24 shrimp.

- ☐ **1 cup finely chopped hazelnuts**

(filberts)
- ☐ **³/₄ cup flaked coconut**
- ☐ **2 teaspoons grated orange zest, orange part of rind only**
- ☐ **¹/₂ teaspoon ground nutmeg**
- ☐ **24 large shrimp, shelled, but with the tails left on and deveined**
- ☐ **¹/₄ cup cornstarch**
- ☐ **1 cup mango purée or puréed chutney**

1   Combine hazelnuts, coconut, orange zest and nutmeg on a sheet of waxed paper, reserve.

2   Split the shrimp almost in half, lengthwise, open like a book and gently flatten.

3   Place the cornstarch in a plastic bag. Add the shrimp and shake the bag until all the shrimp are coated with the cornstarch. Dip in the mango purée and then in the nut mixture; set aside.

4   Meanwhile, heat enough vegetable oil in a large skillet or saucepan to completely submerge the shrimp.

5   Carefully add one third of the shrimp and fry 1 to 2 minutes, or until shrimp are pink. Using tongs or a slotted spoon, carefully remove the shrimp to paper toweling to drain. Repeat with remaining shrimp.

❖ FABULOUS FILLINGS ❖

CARROT AND FETA CHEESE FILLING: Sauté 2 strips finely chopped bacon in a medium-size skillet over moderate-high heat until browned and crisp. Using a slotted spoon, remove the bacon to paper-toweling to drain. Reduce the heat to medium, add 2 green onions, finely chopped and 1 carrot grated, and sauté, stirring occasionally for 2 to 3 minutes. Remove to paper toweling with bacon. Beat 2 eggs slightly in a medium-size bowl. Add ¹/₂ cup milk, 2 ounces (¹/₂ cup) feta cheese, crumbled and 2 ounces (¹/₂ cup) Cheddar cheese, shredded. Stir in bacon, carrot and green onions.

BROCCOLI AND LEMON FILLING: Trim the flowerettes from 2 small stalks broccoli, about ¹/₂ pound; cut into bite-size pieces. Reserve the stems for soup or other use. Bring 1 quart of water to boiling in a large skillet or saucepan. Add broccoli and cook for 3 to 5 minutes, or until tender-crisp. Transfer broccoli to colander and refresh under cold running water. Drain thoroughly. Pat dry with paper toweling. Finely chop and reserve. Beat 2 eggs slightly in a medium-size bowl. Add ¹/₂ cup milk, 2 ounces Swiss or Gruyere cheese, shredded (¹/₂ cup), 2 green onions, finely chopped, 1 teaspoon country Dijon-style mustard and 1 teaspoon grated lemon zest.

FRENCH ONION FILLING: Melt 1 tablespoon butter or margarine in a heavy medium-size skillet over moderate heat until bubbly. Add 3 medium onions, finely chopped (1¹/₂ cups) and sauté, stirring occasionally, 4 to 5 minutes or until golden. Remove from the heat and reserve. Beat 2 eggs slightly in a medium-size bowl. Add ¹/₂ cup plain low-fat yogurt, 1 ounce grated Parmesan cheese (¹/₄ cup) and 2 tablespoons blue cheese, crumbled and ¹/₂ teaspoon ground nutmeg Stir in onion and mix well.

SUGAR AND SPICE

❖ CROQUEMBOUCHE ❖

Makes 25 servings.

PUFFS
- [ ] **2 cups water**
- [ ] **¹/₂ cup (1 stick) butter or margarine, cut up**
- [ ] **1¹/₂ cups unsifted all-purpose flour**
- [ ] **8 eggs**

FILLING
- [ ] **2¹/₂ cups heavy cream**
- [ ] **6 tablespoons IOX (confectioners') sugar**

CARAMEL SAUCE
- [ ] **3 cups sugar**
- [ ] **1¹/₂ cups water**

DECORATION
- [ ] **whole unblanched almonds (candy-coated)**
- [ ] **small ribbon bows**

1   Preheat oven to hot (500°).

2   Prepare the Puffs: Bring water and butter to a rolling boil in a large saucepan.

3   Add flour all at once. Stir vigorously with a wooden spoon until mixture forms a thick smooth ball that leaves sides of pan clean. Remove from heat.

4   Beat in eggs, one at a time, with a wooden spoon or elecric hand mixer until paste is shiny and smooth.

5   Drop paste by well-rounded teaspoonfuls, 1¹/₂-inches apart, on large greased cookie sheets.

6   Bake in preheated hot oven (500°) for 5 minutes; reduce temperature to 350° and bake for 5 minutes or until puffed and golden brown. Cool on a wire rack.

7   Prepare the Filling: Beat cream and sugar in a small mixing bowl until stiff; refrigerate. Using the narrow tip of a basting bulb or a small drinking straw, pierce a small hole in the base of each puff. Re-whip cream if necessary. Using a pastry bag fitted with a small writing tip, pipe a small amount of cream mixture into each puff.

8   Prepare the Caramel Sauce: Combine sugar and water in a medium size heavy saucepan and cook over medium heat without boiling, stirring constantly until sugar dissolves. Bring to a boil and boil rapidly until the mixture turns golden brown.

9   Place 11 puffs in a 9-inch circle on a serving platter and place enough puffs in the center to fill the circle or place a croquembouche cone* on a serving platter. Working quickly and carefully (do not let hot sauce touch skin) dip the base of each puff in the Caramel Sauce and continue, making each ring smaller to form an inverted cone shape about 11-inches tall, or arrange the puffs in layers around the cone. Place almonds between puffs, drizzle over remaining Caramel Sauce and finally decorate with small ribbon bows. Let stand at room temperature in a cool place for up to 6 hours.

❖ MEXICAN WEDDING ❖ COOKIES

This is an adaptation of an original Mexican wedding cookie recipe. The cookies can be made up in advance and stored in airtight containers. Dust with extra IOX (confectioners') sugar before serving.

Makes 2 dozen cookies.

☐ **1 cup (2 sticks) butter or margarine**
☐ **¹/₂ cup sifted IOX (confectioners') sugar**
☐ **1 teaspoon almond extract**
☐ **2 cups sifted all-purpose flour**
☐ **¹/₂ cup finely chopped almonds**
☐ **IOX (confectioners') sugar**

1   Preheat the oven to moderate (350°). Lightly grease 2 large cookie sheets with vegetable shortening. Set aside.
2   Beat together the butter, IOX (confectioners') sugar and almond extract in a large bowl with an electric mixer until light and fluffy. Add the flour and almonds. Beat at low speed until a firm dough forms.

Cover and refrigerate for 30 minutes.
3   Roll dough between the palm of the hands, into balls about 1-inch in diameter. Place 2-inches apart on prepared sheets.
4   Bake in the preheated moderate oven (350°) for 20 minutes or until lightly browned.
5   Remove cookies to wire racks. Roll in IOX (confectioners') sugar while still warm. Return to wire racks to cool completely.
6   Store in airtight containers until ready to serve.

Opposite: Wedding sweets including Croquembouche, Mexican Wedding Cookies, Love Cake. Right: Pistachio and Stilton Grapes

❖ LOVE CAKE ❖

Makes 25 servings.

☐ **8 eggs, separated**
☐ **2¹/₄ cups sugar**
☐ **2 cups ground almonds**
☐ **1¹/₂ cups fine cornmeal**
☐ **4 tablespoons light corn syrup**
☐ **¹/₂ teaspoon grated lemon zest (yellow part of rind only)**
☐ **¹/₂ teaspoon ground nutmeg**
☐ **¹/₂ teaspoon ground cardamom**
☐ **¹/₂ teaspoon almond extract**

1   Preheat oven to slow (300°). Lightly grease and line with wax paper a 8 x 1¹/₂-inch round cake pan. Set aside.
2   Beat the egg yolks in a large bowl with an electric mixer until light and fluffy. Gradually add half of the sugar, beating well after each addition, until creamy.
3   Add ground almonds, flour, water, lemon zest, nutmeg, cardamom and almond extract, stir until well blended.
4   Using clean beaters and another large bowl, beat the egg whites with an electric mixer on high speed until foamy. Gradually beat in remaining sugar a tablespoon at a time until stiff, glossy peaks form.
5   Fold almond mixture into the beaten egg whites until blended. Spoon into the prepared pan.
6   Bake in the preheated slow oven (300°) for 1 hour 30 minutes until golden and a wooden pick inserted in the center comes out clean.
7   Remove pan to wire rack. Gently loosen cake from edge of pan using a thin metal spatula. Cool on the wire rack for 10

minutes. Remove the cake from the pan to the wire rack and cool completely.

❖ PISTACHIO AND ❖ STILTON GRAPES

To serve these delicious morsels arrange them in the shape of a bunch of grapes. If you have either a real or ornamental grape vine, use some of the leaves to decorate the plate.

Makes 30.
☐ **¹/₂ cup (4 ounces) cream cheese, softened**
☐ **¹/₄ cup (2 ounces) Stilton cheese, crumbled**
☐ **2 tablespoons sour cream**
☐ **30 large seedless green grapes**
☐ **¹/₂ cup finely chopped pistachio nuts**

1   Beat cream cheese, Stilton cheese and sour cream in a small bowl until smooth and creamy.
2   Coat grapes with cheese mixture and roll in pistachio nuts to completely cover. Refrigerate until firm.

AND NOW, THE HONEYMOON

You've tossed the bouquet and bid farewell to your guests. Now begins a new life with your spouse. After months of planning and weeks of parties and celebrations with friends and relatives, the honeymoon is just for you. It's the opportunity for romance, relaxation – adventure perhaps – but most importantly for getting to know each other, as husband and wife, before returning to the routine of everyday life.

Planning a honeymoon is not nearly as complicated as planning a wedding, but it does take some work. Make your arrangements, and finalize them, well in advance of the wedding so you'll have smooth sailing after the big day.

Beachcombing on a tropical island may be your idea of the perfect vacation. For others, it may be backpacking through the mountains. (Planning the honeymoon is often the first test of a couple's ability to compromise!)

Decide together where you'll go and how long you'll travel. Pay careful attention to your budget – you don't want to start married life with an empty bank account. Consider all the costs of travel: transportation, accommodations, meals, car rentals, fees and vaccinations, even tips and souvenirs. If you're planning to buy new clothes or luggage for the trip, count that in your budget as well.

Since you may be a little tired

A new life together

Photography by Alan Khan and Christopher Poulos

after the wedding, it can be a good idea to spend your wedding night at a local hotel and leave at your leisure the next day for your well-deserved vacation.

Make the travel arrangements yourself or go through a travel agent. Try to choose the option that presents the fewest headaches.

If you're planning to travel overseas, you'll need a passport. Apply for your passport as early as possible through your local passport office or post office. It can take several weeks for your application to be processed, so plan far in advance. If you already hold a passport, you may

have it amended to include your married name. Contact the passport office or post office for more information.

For overseas travel, it is best to take your money in the form of traveler's checks which are available from most banks. You'll also need a small amount of local currency for taxis, tips and incidentals. Foreign currency is available at some banks, or at the airport upon your arrival.

Travel insurance can protect you against loss of money paid in advance for tickets and accommodations, loss of baggage, extra expenses if you are delayed by a strike or natural disaster, and medical expenses. You might want to consider taking insurance on your trip.

Pack light, but efficiently. Be sure to take at least one pair of walking shoes and a pair of dress shoes for the evening. For most destinations, women can get by with a jacket, jeans, shorts and T-shirts, a couple of blouses, a swimsuit and one or two uncrushable dresses. Men should pack sports clothes, shorts and T-shirts, a sweater, swim trunks, and a sports coat and tie for the evening.

Enjoy the time you have alone together on your honeymoon. Relax and unwind after the excitement of the big day. Savor the memory of your wedding day, and look ahead to a long and happy life together.

THANK YOU

We would like to thank the following generous individuals and companies who assisted in the preparation of this book: The Australia East India Company for supplying the beautiful glasses; Australian Squatters Company of Willoughby, New South Wales for supplying garden accessories; Sharon Blain for the very clever hair styling; Canning Vale Spinning Mills, Sydney for supplying our lovely cotton towels; Stephen Clarke for creating the Heart-Shaped Wedding Cake; Cottage and Lace for the hand-painted pots and sunhat; the Fish Marketing Authority for providing the prawns and lobster; Home Yardage, New South Wales for the plain fabrics; Liberty for supplying all our pretty printed fabrics; Lifestyle Imports and Limoges for the beautiful china; Leo Lynch and Sons of Flemington Markets, New South Wales for the lovely flowers; McCalls Patterns for their Heritage Trims; Myer Australia for the Vogue pattern wedding dress no.1519; N.Z. Berries for providing the berries; Offray for the wonderful ribbons; Pat Ray for creating the Tiered Wedding Cake; Royal Atlantic Salmon for supplying the smoked salmon; Julia Stewart of Lindfield for her expert assistance with make-up and beauty advice; Sydney Rock Oysters for supplying the oysters; R. P. Symonds for the beautiful crystal and silverware; Village Pharmacy, Lindfield, New South Wales for lending bathroom accessories; Wendy B's florists of Mosman, New South Wales for the wedding bouquet.

We would also like to thank Admiral Appliances; Black & Decker (Australasia) Pty Ltd; Blanco Appliances; Knebel Kitchens; Leigh Mardon Pty Ltd; Master Foods of Australia; Meadow Lea Foods; Namco Cookware; Sunbeam Corporation Ltd; Tycraft Pty Ltd, distributors of Braun Australia and White Wings Foods.

INDEX

FOOD INDEX